Only Gone From Your Sight

Jack McAfghan's
Little Guide to Pet Loss and Grief

Kate McGahan LMSW

This book is a supplement, not a substitute for medical/psychological care or grief support. The reader should consult a health care professional in matters relating to his/her health, particularly with respect to any symptoms that may require diagnosis or medical attention.

**I dedicate this book
to children of all ages and everywhere
who have ever loved a pet with all their heart
and soul.**

*I am not gone
Just Gone from Sight.
In the blink of an eye
I'll see you again
When the time is just right.
Wipe the tears from your eyes
And watch for the signs that I send to remind you
That Love Never Dies.*

OTHER BOOKS BY KATE McGAHAN

THE JACK McAFGHAN PET LOSS TRILOGY

Book I
Jack McAfghan Reflections on Life with my Master
A Dog's Memoir on Life After Death
Read Jack's story and start healing your heart by
the final page. Our story is your story too.

Book 2
The Lizard from Rainbow Bridge:
The True Tale of an Unexpected Angel
Mr. Lizard will help you to recognize the signs that
are all around you.

Book 3
Return from Rainbow Bridge:
An Afterlife Story of Love, Loss and Renewal
Open your mind to the possibilities that exist in
life after death.

It's Not Putting Me Down It's Lifting Me Up
A Guilt-Free Guide to End of Life Decisions for
Pets
(pertinent excerpts from "Only Gone from your Sight"
to specifically assist with end of life animal care)

Sign up at http://www.KateMcGahan.com to
receive updates on upcoming book releases!

Preface

Author Kate McGahan had been an end of life counselor for three decades when she lost her heart and soul dog Jack, an eight-year-old mixed breed Afghan hound. When Jack passed on their kitchen floor four days following a surgical procedure, she was put to the test. Less than 24 hours after his passing she received a call that her father had died too, unexpectedly. It began an emotional and spiritual journey that would force the professional to work through her own personal grief and to transform herself through the power of love over loss.

Six months later, during one of many insomniac nights of the soul, Jack came to her. She dusted off her bedside journal which had been untouched since his death and she began to write. The pages she wrote that night, written to her from Jack's canine perspective, would be the beginning of the first book. Two more books in the Trilogy would follow.

This fourth book in the Jack McAfghan series has been thoughtfully designed with short chapters and diverse presentation. It will answer questions you might have about the end of life and questions you have not even thought of asking yet. Throughout, excerpts from the Trilogy are featured. If you have a chance, please read the very first book, "Reflections". Jack will take you in storybook fashion through your grief and out the other side to healing.

Just as Kate helped thousands over the years with their grief, Jack would come to help her through hers. He comes to you now to help you to heal your heart too.

Gone From My Sight

I am standing upon the seashore.
A ship, at my side,
spreads her white sails to the moving breeze
and starts for the blue ocean.
She is an object of beauty and strength.
I stand and watch her until, at length,
she hangs like a speck
of white cloud just where the sea and sky
come to mingle with each other.
Then, someone at my side says,
"There, she is gone."
Gone where?

Gone from my sight. That is all.

She is just as large in mast,
hull and spar as she was when she left my side.
And, she is just as able
to bear her load of living freight
to her destined port.
Her diminished size is in me -- not in her.
And, just at the moment when someone says,
"There, she is gone,"
there are other eyes watching her coming,
and other voices ready to take up the glad shout,
"Here she comes!"

...And that is dying...

~Written in 1904 by Henry Van Dyke (1852-1933)

Table of Contents

INTRODUCTION

Dear One,

I see how you are grieving. You think your heart is broken and that you will never be happy again. You are facing the loss of someone near and dear to you and it happens to be your pet. Those who never loved a pet the way you have loved yours cannot fathom the magnitude of it. This is a unique once-in-a-lifetime love affair rooted in trust, loyalty, acceptance without conditions; love without limits. All the time. Forever and ever.

You think no one understands, but I do. My name is Jack. I was born in a puppy mill and I never dreamed I would have a beautiful life, but I sure did! I was so lucky the day she came through the gate and chose me. I was only 10 weeks old and the day I met her my life changed forever. Those of us who have had a loving home with a best friend who loves us as much as we love them, we are blessed! I know that you are one of those loving people because that is why you are reading this book. I know you are missing your pet with all your heart and soul and that you came here to find peace and understanding in your loss. You are reading this book because you have loved and been loved so much and you wonder how you'll make it through the grief.

As you all too well know, it is one of the most difficult things in a human lifetime to say goodbye to a loyal best friend. Stay with me here and I will prove to you that it's not goodbye at all. It's not the end.

Join me on a guided tour through the world of grief. In the pages that follow I will help you to prepare for inevitable loss and difficult end of life decisions. Together we'll travel through the five stages of grief. We will discuss memorial ideas, the power of signs and dreams; how to talk with your children and other pets about the loss and how to move forward into living life fully, perhaps even opening your heart to love again.

I will be referring to the words "Dead" "Death" "Die" and "Dying". I do it for the sake of simplicity but the fact is if you have read my other books you know there is no such thing as death. My definition of death is not the death of the spirit but the freeing of the spirit of the soul. The soul is what lives on long beyond this earthly life. It is the part of each one of us that lives forever. It is connected to everyone we love no matter what, no matter where we are.

As your Rainbow Bridge representative, please join me on this special journey. Don't be surprised if you feel the presence of your best friend here with us, for we are all here beside you, only gone from your view as you read these words, as you cry your tears and one day as you smile your gentle smile for the memory of us. We bring you the comfort of a friend who loves and supports you no matter what. There is no judgment here. There is no criticism. There is only love and understanding. We are devoted to you forever. We are never far away. It's our turn to take you for a little walk...along the edge of the Rainbow. Come. Everything is going to be okay. You'll see.

Love, Jack

IF YOU WERE A FLOWER
THE NATURAL CYCLE OF LIFE

Nature continually reminds us of the natural cycles of life. If you were a flower, when the harshness of winter comes you would pull yourself deep inside to protect yourself from freezing, to prevent yourself from dying. You toughen up the outside, close yourself up and go deep within where you are always safe.

Then after quite a long while there comes a bit of warmth and a welcoming day brings with it the thaw. Spring comes and something inside of you stirs. You realize you've survived another winter. The ice melts away and you can feel the outside of yourself again. As the warmth so long gone from your life surrounds you, you decide maybe it's worth blooming again for another season. Hope returns to your heart as you prepare for new life.

You begin to open again as the sun fuels your soul. Your energy returns. An infusion of life force comes to you, giving you more power than you have known since you went into hibernation. This power is the force that pushes you to develop your stems, to press through the soil, to stretch forth and reach towards the light again.

Sometimes Spring can make you an April fool, bringing a bluff! What you planned on, the rain that waters your roots so that you can grow again, turns unexpectedly to ice then snow and it finds you unsuspecting. You are vulnerable and alone, exposed and unprotected. Your tender life is threatened. In some seasons the storm will pass quickly and you will survive; other seasons you can be hurt so deeply that you must withdraw and retreat deep into your roots where you will take the remaining seasons off to rebuild yourself and prepare for the distant day when Spring returns and gives you another chance to thrive.

Despite everything in this year you have survived and in the next season you will grow hardy and beautiful, thriving for the harshness that once threatened you. The early blooms that sprouted, only to be frozen, pinched back by Nature Herself, are destined to return brighter and stronger than ever.

This is the YOU that has grown from the cold harsh winter of your loss. You are the flower that is destined to bloom again. You are the root. You are the bloom. You are the spirit; you are the soul that lives inside every living thing. With each passing season you become stronger and wiser. You go deeper and deeper within where your power can be found. Your roots reach further and further into the quiet nourishing protective earthy space that surrounds you. Look how far you've come from being the fragile shoot that first made itself known in the landscape of life!

Your colorful blooms will burst forth stretching now to the sky and you'll show no fear because you know that no matter what happens you will adjust to the climate that surrounds you and you will be okay. It's what you've learned.

And so it goes.

4

DEATH:
FEARED & MISUNDERSTOOD

"Why are people so afraid of death?
Why do they avoid talking about it?
Maybe it's because there are no words.
With my limited knowledge of the English language,
There is not a word I have ever heard
That accurately describes what "death" is.
You can look it up in the dictionary for yourself.
I don't believe what they say it is.
How can you say death is death
When it is not death at all, but life?
Reflections, Chapter 53

Death is one of the top fears in society. Statistically, collective fears tend to change with the times. Things are shifting dramatically in this day and age. People are becoming more highly aware of the power of politics and the seriousness of global issues; awareness made possible through high-speed technology and the media. More and more people are finding themselves fearing the End of the Global World or the next financial collapse. Many who never lived through the Great Depression, the wars, the tougher times, never worried much about these issues. After all, you don't tend to worry about things unless they touch you personally. There is a certain natural denial if you have never experienced such things; you think you are immune to them. You are not immune but you can count your blessings.

Regardless, the top fears of most people are: Fear of dependency in old age, fear of public speaking and fear of death. Death was coming in at #3 last time we checked. Public speaking actually was coming in first for a while. Most people apparently would rather die than give a public speech.

You live in a society that typically fears death, avoids tears and suppresses anger. Humans have a tendency to hide all of these things away. You don't share them freely. You don't express them. You don't show them. You tend to deny them. Because you hold them inside yourself, over time and circumstance they can wreak havoc on your bodies, minds and relationships.

Most portrayals of death in the media can be disturbing at best. Many people grew up as children fearing the dark, along with the ghosts and goblins and monsters that lived under their beds. They quickly learned to fear death too. The beautiful souls and spirits of those who love them became creepy and unwelcome phantoms. Many are now adults and are still so scared that they haven't yet thought to look to see if there is a monster under the bed at all. They are so anxious about death that they close the door in haste and shut death on the other side. They never learn that life goes on; the souls of their loved ones living forever in a sacred place where they wait for everyone else to join them some day in a land where love never dies. These children become adults who have lost faith in what they cannot see. Knowledge is power and people tend to fear that which they do not understand. They forget that they are never ever separated --- no not even by death -- from the ones they love.

Oh if you could only see the beauty that is on the other side! There are no grim reapers, there are only spiritual beings made of love. But you don't know that yet. You begin worrying about the loss of someone long before loss is ever an issue. You live from fear instead of from love. You cling because you don't want to lose them, knowing that one day, someday, they will die. You spoil the clarity of love and the experience of your relationship in the meantime by clinging to the dependence and neediness that is triggered by your fears of the future. Ultimately you miss out on the best parts of life.

One of the things we come to teach you is how to live and love in the moment. It is one of the things pets, and all animals actually, do best. Love and fear cannot coexist in the same space. I want you to live in the moment because Love lives in the moment and I don't want you to be afraid anymore. When you live in the moment and put your love for me first, fear cannot exist. So if you are afraid, you must take a look at yourself and see where it is that love is lacking. Stop looking back and stop looking ahead and look at where you are right now. Then turn up the love so loud that fear cannot be heard over the voice of love. I will tell you later in this book how to do it.

When you hold your feelings deep inside, longstanding anger and resentments can rear their heads. They surface and are magnified tenfold in your grief. Yet you hide your tears. You continue to fear death because nobody wants to

7

talk about it for very long. Nobody talks about it but it is the one thing the dying need. It is the one thing the grieving need. It is what you need now. To be able to talk about what it is like to experience the most shared and commonly feared human event on earth: death and the fear of the Great Unknown.

A highly trained experienced hospice worker can be very good at serving the dying and their families. While important, it is not so much the college degree or expertise that makes a worker good. It is their responsiveness, combined with the humble willingness and ability to listen and To Be Present In The Moment that makes the difference in the quality of the death experience. Anyone can do it and not many do. Many people simply don't know how to live in the moment even when the precious moments before death come calling.

The dying yearn to talk about their experience. To share their last full range of feelings and thoughts. To touch the ones they love in body, mind and spirit. They want desperately to share what they see, what they feel, what they've learned, how they've loved. It is the greatest adventure in life, death, and yet so many loved ones reply to them, "Oh don't talk that way," because they themselves are afraid of death and helplessly uncomfortable with the topic.

The best thing you can do is to become familiar with death so that when someone needs you to be present with them you are not so filled with your own fear and discomfort that you cannot be. You will be able to practice what I taught you in our days together. To live in the moment so you can share in the moment with

8

those who need your love and attention. You will not only be better prepared when that day comes for you, but you can give your loved ones what they need when the time comes for them. It's one of the reasons we wrote this book. So that you won't be afraid anymore.

Are you getting the support you need from others in your grief? Keep in mind that it stands to reason that if most people avoid talking about anger and/or the topic of death, chances are they will avoid you too when you are angry or when you are grieving or when you are dying. Most have no idea what to say to you because they have no experience, no training, and no practice. If you are dying, longing to connect with them as you hear their hushed whispers behind the hospital curtain, you are already feeling more alone. Already it is as if you are not there. It is like a preview of the future. It helps you to see what it will be like after death when you are in the room with them, beyond the curtain, beyond the veil, and they don't realize you are there. They turn away now from your deathbed, thinking they are helping you, protecting you from some truth they have come up with. You will have your work cut out for you: to find a way to teach them and show them what is true. To believe in what they cannot see.

If you are grieving you may find yourself feeling alone for similar reasons. Many people will be overwhelmed with the discomfort that comes with seeing your tears, feeling your anger and not wanting to think about death. The presence of death only reminds them of their own mortality and fears surrounding loss or eventual loss of

9

their own loved ones. It's like they are in a state of denial even now as you stand before them in your pain. Some will avoid you. Some will try to jolt you out of it and change the subject. They might say something completely inappropriate or try to be funny or come across sarcastic or rude. While you have been pushed from behind into the deep end of the pool of life, they will stand at the surface trying to keep things shallow as they talk about the weather or other trivial things designed to enable them to stay within their own comfort zones. Any discomfort they feel is triggered by yours and they are desperate to diffuse it and most don't know how.

Meanwhile you are potentially shattering their illusion by showing them once again that death keeps coming around. No one will escape it. Not even them. Soon you will help them to see what I have come to teach you. Soon they will find out that there is nothing to fear. They will learn that love never dies. The soul never dies. They will learn that the only thing that dies is death.

NO LIFE WITHOUT LOSS

Every loss in life is a type of death. You will go through thousands of large and little deaths in your lifetime. Whether it is the death of someone close to you or perhaps a divorce or loss of a job or a certain status, every loss brings with it the need to grieve. The distress of grief is very real. Don't let anyone tell you it isn't. Just like you need to recover from an illness or a broken bone, there's a recovery period to heal the invisible wounds of grief.

Grief is an emotional roller coaster. You will have your ups and downs and moments of terror and brief moments of peace. You can only go as fast as the ride will take you. You will manage it in your own way, either clinging to the edge in panic and fear or raising your hands into the sky and embracing the ride as it takes you around the curves, dips and flights of riveting emotion. Either way, it has your full attention. You can think of nothing else. Somewhere in between these extremes is where you will grieve. You will choose how you will do it. It's the only choice you have right now. Just remember: the ride will end and you will be okay.

Grief is a very personal thing but it has a fairly predictable course. In 1969, renowned psychiatrist and death expert extraordinaire Elisabeth Kübler-

Ross introduced her theory that most people can expect to go through various stages of grieving. They do it in their own way and in their own time. She outlined five stages: Denial, Anger, Bargaining, Depression and Acceptance. We will be discussing them here in this book. We will also be discussing guilt because there is really no grief without guilt. Guilt, shame and blame run rampant throughout the grief process and are often the most challenging parts in healing for someone who is still learning to live in the world in peace.

The five stages are just a guide. If you have lost anything in your life, and I know you have, you might be amazed when you look back on it now how you went through all or most of these stages. From misplaced sentimental items to the breakup of a relationship; from losing a job to losing a loved one, to coping with having a terminal illness or a permanent disability, the five stages are a guide to the typical process an individual goes through to come to terms with loss.

When does grief begin? Grief does not wait for actual death. Grief can seep into your being as soon as loss becomes a certain and foreseeable reality. This is the beginning of a unique and personal journey. There is no normal. You never know how long it will take to heal. Try not to compare your experience with someone else's. Please don't stand in judgment of yourself and pay no heed to someone who thinks you are not grieving "the right way".

You will need time to go through your own version of grief. Ross's structure provides some comfort in the storm of loss because it helps to validate your feelings along the way. It helps you to see that you are not the only one experiencing these thoughts and emotions. It reassures you that there is a timeline for grief and an inevitable evolution and personal transformation that will take place because of it. You will go through the process in your own time in your own way and at your own pace. This book will help you to understand the process but it's ultimately up to you how long it will take. Some take a few months or less or more. Some take many years. Some never allow themselves to heal at all. There are some who are able to let grief have its way with them, allowing things to be what they are with hardly a tear. There is no "right way" to grieve. There is no "wrong way" to grieve. There is only YOUR way.

Do you believe in an afterlife? If you do this book will make more sense to you. Some people do, some people don't. Some people have had near death experiences that have proven to them beyond a doubt that life exists beyond this earthly life. Others believe that the end of this life is the end of everything. Perhaps you believe in the resurrection or the reincarnation of a soul over many lifetimes. Perhaps you don't believe in Heaven. Or Hell. Or maybe you do. If you are a scientist you probably scoff at the idea of pets crossing the Rainbow Bridge but still you know that energy cannot die, it only changes form and love is energy so therefore you know that it's true that love can never die.

Everyone is different. Every relationship is different. Every life is different. Cultures create diverse perspectives. Religions carve out different kinds of rules and beliefs. Different people grieve differently.

That said, sorrow is a universal feeling. Like a smile or a tear, even if someone does not speak your language, they understand it when they witness it. Many people are intimately familiar with the sorrow of grief; there are just different ways of dealing with it from culture to culture, person to person. It's important not to judge someone based on faith, cultural traditions or beliefs. You have yours, they have theirs and nobody is right or wrong.

Animals live without creed or religion. These concepts hold no meaning for us. Our "religion" is only love. We need no creed or commandment for we always do the right thing because we always live from acceptance and from the love in our hearts. We have faith in life after death. It is a priority for us to be loyal to our master. We have had you as master upon the earth and we return home to our Master in Heaven. We knew this when we arrived and we know this when it's time to leave. No matter what side of the rainbow we are on, we never forget the one we belong to or where our forever home is.

NOT 'JUST' A PET

It was hard for friends to know how to comfort her. After all, I had been like her child, her boyfriend, her husband and her best friend all wrapped up in one furry package. Pets can become like family members especially for those who do not have a family of their own.
Reflections, Chapter 73

You might find it difficult to open up your heart and talk with most people because you fear they might think you crazy for loving me more than you've loved any human. All too many who deeply grieve the loss of a pet have been 'reassured' by a statement from a well-meaning friend, "It's just a dog/ cat/ horse/ hamster/ rabbit/ parakeet... You can get another one." Forgive them for they know not what they do or what they say.

Even other animal owners might not understand. Some people who own pets are only master, not friend, and they miss out on the best parts of the human-animal bond. If only they could see that we are there to teach them and to give them the love that has otherwise been missing in their lives. The love most humans do not know how to give...or receive. These are the people who might laugh or sneer at you now when you call me your soulmate because they never have heard of such a thing. They think that all soulmates are romantic relationships between two people, not loving relationships between two beings, two friends, two soul travelers such as us. Pity them for what they do not know. Pity them that they cannot treat anyone else better than they treat themselves. Pity them for the love they've never had or recognized.

Love is chemistry beyond our control. When true love comes into your life it can transform you in the most extraordinary ways and change everything you ever believed in. You are never sure where true love is going to come from and it can be quite a surprise when it comes from your pet.

While it may sound strange that someone can grieve more deeply for a pet than for a human, there is a certain undeniable depth that comes from sharing a life of unconditional love. It doesn't matter how many legs I have or how many you have, it's a soul connection. No matter how we found each other, no matter how long we have been together, it is a relationship like no other. I have given you the kind of love that takes humans a lifetime to learn, if they ever learn. I know the power of love and I want to give it to you. It is the most powerful force in the universe. I came into this world to give true love to you and to draw true love out of you. How many people in your life do that?

Of course people do the best they can, giving and receiving their imperfect human love. There are a few special people on earth who are very old souls and they are capable of loving at a very deep level. They give the highest form of love; love that is divinely pure, honest and unconditional. It holds the loved one more precious than oneself. It sacrifices without complaint, without resentment, without keeping score. It gives and gives and expects nothing in return. It's the same kind of love that I have given to you. I came into the world to love and be loved and I chose you. Love is why I came here. You are the reason I came. My love has become a part of you but you don't seem to understand that yet. When I am gone you don't seem to know who you are without me. You don't know your identity without me. I will teach you. I will teach you through life and I will teach you through death. I will teach you that love never dies.

When you love from the depths of the soul in your heart, you are never apart from the one you love no matter how far away you seem to be. Even when I am gone from your sight, I am never gone from your heart. We live in the heart of one another for eternity, beyond the reaches of this world. The love runs deep. That's why it hurts so much for so long when we have to say "goodbye". That's also why you will get through this. Our love runs so deep that nothing can touch it, no, not even death. Our love will win. It always does when it is true.

I tried to comfort her. I spoke in a voice she could not hear. Her grief and sadness drowned me out. I wanted to tell her what I have always known. That life is but a dream leading to love. Love, more powerful than her fear could ever be.
Love cannot be destroyed. It grows and grows until it is stronger than death.
Reflections, Chapter 72

Soulmates change all the rules in the game of life. We have been brought together, you and me, by a common destiny. We have known each other before and we will know each other again. I will continue to transform you from beyond the grave and help you to see that love is more valuable and powerful than anything else.

There will be others who will not understand this kind of love. They will raise their eyebrows as they stand in judgment of you and comment how silly it is that you loved me this much. Don't worry about them. I feel sorry for them. They obviously have never encountered a soulmate of their own or they would know better. They would know that traditional rules do not apply when a match is made in Heaven. Once you know this kind of love you will never question love again. You'll know it when you see it. You'll know it when you feel it. You will never be confused by something that is something else.

ANTICIPATORY GRIEF
FACING THE INEVITABLE

Death. I wish the word could be removed from the vocabulary and from the dictionary. It simply does not exist, except in the human mind that was taught that it does exist. People think they are a body and they come to believe that when the body dies, everything they are will die too. It's not true. The soul lives on. The soul of consciousness exists not only in the body but outside of the body too. We are all souls that cannot be contained or limited by time or space or the physical body. For souls there is no death.

Return from Rainbow Bridge, Chapter 13

When you brought me into your life it changed everything for both of us. It was not so long ago we were still traveling the world together thinking we'd live forever.

All the adventures come to pass and then seemingly out of the blue one day something happens that, once again, changes everything. Life will never be the same. The fear sets in. The threat of loss permeates your being and taints the world around you, disrupting everything. It's all you can think about, the impending loss of me. It's another kind of adventure that we will come to share. When something big changes your life, it's because you have something big to learn. You learned from my coming and you'll learn from my going.

Living with fear and the ache in your heart as you watch me decline, you wonder how you'll ever live without me. Perhaps you have already made some difficult choices on my behalf. Costly medications. Challenging treatments. Surgeries. Countless fears and days and nights on end filled with worry for me.

You look back on the investment of life you have made with me. From the early training to the bond of love we've created through life's ups and downs, you've became a part of me and I've become a part of you. That bond of love we've created together will never be broken even though I will soon be gone. Oh but not gone at all, Only Gone From Your Sight.

Anticipatory grief begins the moment you realize that my death is inevitable, that there's no going back to the way things used to be. You will probably go through a mini-version of the five stages of grief during this pre-grief process, during your anticipation of what is ahead. Your life shifts dramatically because you now anticipate my death and must prepare for it. But how on earth do you prepare for something such as this?

"Oh no no no," you Deny. "It cannot be true!" You are Angry. "It's just not fair!" You Bargain. "Certainly there must be more tests that can be done!" You become Depressed when you learn that there are no more tests; there is nothing that can be done. There is little time left.

You learn that you have no control over the situation and you are ultimately forced to accept the circumstances. You imagine your world without me in it. Hesitantly you begin to picture what your life will be like and, while unpleasant, the visualization of it is like a little rehearsal. It's like a preview that prepares you just a little bit for when the time comes. It's all predesigned so that you can begin to accept the fact that I am dying.

Some of you begin this process of grief long before there is need for concern. This usually stems from your fear of the future, your attachment to me, and an ultimate Not Wanting and Not Knowing What To Do when the time comes. It stems from the fear that you can't make it on your own without me. It's the resistance of having to face the living of life without me in it. Death forces change. It's the final stage of growth for the one who is dying and it is a teacher that forces the growth of the one who remains. Most people are averse to change and they tend to cling to old ways of being in an effort to try to keep things the same. But they can't keep things the same. So they grieve just thinking about it.

It isn't necessarily healthy, the clinging and this feeling of need that you have, but it's understandable. This early phase is by design. It gives you time. It makes you extra appreciative of what you have now. I am so grateful because I know you always appreciated me, but when you know the end of something is coming, you don't take anything for granted. When you know your time is short, each moment is precious and with each moment comes the opportunity to say what needs to be said and to express your deepest love and appreciation to the one who will be leaving soon. Or to the one who loves the one who is leaving soon, if you happen to be the one who is dying.

Believe it or not, this anticipatory time is a gift in disguise. Not everyone is given time to prepare for loss. Some experience loss through trauma, accident, or sudden death. It happens so fast that you don't know what hit you. You never had a chance to say goodbye. You could not have anticipated it. There was no way to prepare for it. You did not have the "luxury" of this phase of experience called Anticipatory Grief.

If you have not learned this, we now have this opportunity for me to teach you to look at your life and mine In The Moment. To help you to see what you have now and what you will not have later and to make the most of each and every moment we have together in the meantime.

I've been waiting for you. Come with me. Let's live In The Moment together...

PRE-GRIEF

We've received the diagnosis and it's not good news. There's no hope for survival. It's overwhelming and it takes only a moment to overload your mind. You can feel so blindsided at the time that you stop functioning. You just do whatever you are told to do. This phenomenon often takes place at the veterinarian's office when the diagnosis, with poor prognosis, is first presented. Being overwhelmed by it is not your fault; it's the shock of the situation. You nod your head and passively say, "Okay" to everything. Even the things you don't quite understand. You don't make the most of communicating your feelings, stating your needs or asking your questions. There's nothing more that can be done. You see no way out; you're between a rock and a hard place. You don't ask how much it will cost. You don't learn the remaining options or alternatives. You are thrown into a state of shock and denial, blinded like a deer in headlights.

Fear takes over. You come to look at everything through the filter of your fear and you feel disempowered. You find you can't make clear decisions and you default to someone, anyone, who will make those decisions for you. You feel that you have lost control and you give it over to the only one who seems willing to take it. You give it to the one with the clearest mind. The expert. The one we have come to trust over our years together. Our veterinarian.

Pre-grief is already kicking in, the shock, the numbness. You're not yourself. You don't think and act the way you normally would. The problem is that later on, you will feel guilty because you won't understand why you didn't have the strength or the know-how to fight the decision or to express your preferences. The shock has disempowered you and you may even feel anger towards the one who encouraged you to make the particular decision, all because you couldn't...even though you agreed to it.

You go into a state of pre-grief shock because you realize that everything is different now. Most things are out of your hands. You have already Shut Down. You aren't up for a fight. You are too overwhelmed trying to figure out how to surrender to things that are beyond your control. For some of you, all that's left is the power of prayer and the hope for a miracle.

You've always been so busy but our days together here are winding down now. The wonderful thing for me is that once you slow down and really focus on what is going on between you and me, you are finally Living In The Moment. I've been trying to teach you this all of my life while your busy world kept you spinning.

The most important thing you can do for me in these final days is to sit quietly with me. BE with me. If we have not already learned how to speak Heart to Heart, we can learn now. Because I do not have a voice to tell you, my heart will help your heart to know what I want and what I need in the days ahead. This is the "language" we can practice now. This is the language that will ultimately help us to transcend the space between us when I am gone from your sight. It's how I will speak to you. It's how I always spoke to you but you never really heard me because you didn't know how. You weren't tuned in. Let's learn now. We will get through this together with the power of the love in our hearts. We have time.

Let's practice. Put one hand on my heart and the other on yours. Sit quietly with me, breathe with me, feel our hearts beating together. Look into my eyes. If I have already made my transition, call me to come to you anyway and I will. Sit with me even though I am gone from your sight. I am still with you; sit with me now. We are building a foundation of understanding, heart to heart. It will be good for both of us. The heart is the bridge that connects us now and it is the bridge that will connect us when I am gone. The bridge that joins your heart to mine IS the Rainbow Bridge!

Someday whenever the world gets to be too much, even when I'm gone, put your hands on your heart because that is where I will be. I will remind you that your power is in your heart, not in your head.

END OF LIFE DECISIONS

WHAT IS NOT GROWING IS DYING

I learned that Blanca felt totally helpless. She was tired of living. She wanted to be free of her cumbersome body. She felt trapped. She loved her family but she suffered from a deep and painful longing to return Home. Her heavenly Master was calling for her but her earthly master was clinging to her. It was painful for her to be pulled in two different directions. She knew that I would understand.
Reflections, Chapter 52

It can be quite surreal, the time before death, when you know for certain that our time together will be brief. The anticipation of the inevitable change is typically harder than the change itself because anticipating something keeps you in the fear of the future. There is a fairly reliable process that must take place. There is a road that we must now travel.

The clock of earthly life ticks off our remaining moments together. We have reached the point where you must make some big decisions on my behalf. It is a precious time for you and me: the final days, hours, minutes, moments...It is a time of shared learning through new feelings and experience. It is my final opportunity to teach you the importance of living with me in the moment. There are so few moments left. I will help you to make the most of every bit of time we have together. It is a time to share our love and affection and it is a time to communicate, your heart to mine, my heart to yours. Like I taught you.

Ask me what I want. I will tell you. You can see the way I carry myself. You can see it in my eyes. It's the light that shines out at you from them that will tell you everything you need to know. My love for you has kept my eyes clear and bright for a very long time. If you see that my eyes have dimmed, it's because some of my light is already shining on the other side of the rainbow. It is because I am preparing for my departure to a forever land where love never dies. Where you and I will ultimately come together to live for eternity.

As I decline, death will probably not take me all at once. You may find that I leave a little bit at a time. Maybe I won't be so steady on my feet or I get so tired that I just can't stay awake without falling asleep again. It is a message to you that I am increasingly "tired" of living this way. I might start having accidents in the house because my systems are shutting down. When I stop eating towards the end of life, it is often my way of telling you to "stop" too. It is the one thing I still have control over, whether I eat or not. It's the one clear way I can communicate with you that I do not want to keep nourishing a life that no longer works for me. There is a different kind of nourishment I need now. As much as I love you,

28

the time comes when we have to give up the fight and surrender to the next journey.

Just like the light in my eyes will tell you if I am leaving, my mind might stray to the other side too. I will be less focused on what is going on around me, more focused on where it is that I am going. You'll look at me and it may seem as if I am not there, but I am. I am just learning some important things from those on the other side who need to speak, their heart to mine, to help me to know what I can expect as I make my transition. Even if my eyes are not focused upon you, I am still here. I am still very aware of your presence and your state of mind. I can still hear you. I can hear you and feel you through all the final moments and beyond...even if I seem to be unconscious.

...Another shift takes place. Your heart is in your throat because you see my eyes have lost their shine. My light has dimmed. You are now observing each and every detail. Your heart sags with sadness within your chest. You're bracing yourself because now you know that it's true. Now you know that I will be leaving you soon. I am already separating from the pain and oh it feels so much better.

Suddenly you are intensely aware of how little control you have. You fast-forward your mind wondering how you will get through this. The fears come. Fears for you. Fears for me. Once again you move out of the love and into the fear. You forget about living in the moment and instead you worry about the future; you fear what is coming. You don't know what to do or how you'll handle it. You think you are not qualified to make end of life decisions for me. They are tough decisions that weigh heavy. You feel that my life is in your hands. You don't want to make these choices all by yourself. You don't need to.

Consult with our veterinarian who will present all the possibilities for my treatment and care. Make sure it can't be fixed. Explore natural remedies. Be open to traditional care. If you are more comfortable getting a second opinion, get a second opinion. Do whatever you can to preserve my comfort and my quality of life. Don't go into a lot of debt to try to save me through expensive procedures, especially if I am older and have been slowing down anyway. I will be saved soon enough when I make my journey into Heaven.

If our vet has done everything possible and my quality of life is still compromised, I must depend on you to decide what's best for me. Put yourself in my place. How does it feel to live like this? In the garden of life what is not growing is dying. So if I am declining, a decision to prolong my life is really only prolonging my dying. If I am running low and my quality of life is compromised, please be willing to let me go. You will understand this more if you have experienced the pain and discomfort that can come with age or if you have ever sought relief from your own pain because of disease or injury. There are worse things than to cross the bridge into the peace that is Heaven. In fact, there is really nothing better. I know it's hard for you to face my death. It's harder for you than it is for me. I am not grieving. You are. You do not grieve for me; you grieve for you for the loss of me. There is no loss in this scenario for me. I will have the peace that is Heaven and I will still have you. I will have everything.

It takes love to hold on when you want to let go. It takes love to let go when you want to hold on. As we move forward together, tell me you love me. Tell me you'll miss me. Tell me you'll grieve and that you will also heal. Reassure me that you'll try to love again. Leave nothing unsaid. Stay by my side whenever possible. Most of all be willing to let me go when it's time to let me go. Give me permission to go so that it is easier for me.

Explore the possibility of care through a pet hospice if there is one in your area. They are invaluable and they will do everything possible to keep me comfortable through my final days. They will also help you to oversee the aftercare arrangements and support you through the process. The thought of having someone there for you even now comforts me. I don't ever want you to feel alone.

If I cannot go on my own terms, I trust you to help me. I know you'll do the right thing when you listen to your heart. The ideal time to let me go is before chronic pain further compromises my quality of life. Let me go on my passage before I have too much pain, before I lose my dignity, before I suffer and create memories of suffering. Those are the memories your mind will tend to go to first and those are the memories I do not want you to focus on. I want you to remember the good times, the healthy happy times when we were in our prime. Oh there were so many of them!

Because it's not your area of expertise, death and letting go, you might think that you need a mediator to help you to make the final decision. The truth is, I am your point of expertise. Nobody knows me like you do. You can hire a good communicator, pet whisperer or counselor...or you can do it yourself. Have you forgotten? You and me, heart to heart? You forgot because you moved out of the moment with me and back into the fear.

Shhhh. Be with me now. Quietly look into my eyes for they will speak to you. The eyes are the windows to the soul; your soul is directly connected to mine. That fact will never change. Tune into my soul and you will know how I feel. The soul understands everything, one for the other. I will show you that I want to stay or let you know if it's time for me to go. Keep the focus on the love in your heart not the fear in your head. Put yourself in my place. I know you love me. Every situation is different and you must do what you must do for you and for me. I have always trusted you to do what is best for me within the choices that we have.

I may have four legs or wings or scales or fins but I understand everything, my heart to yours. Make the most of this time for when all is said and done these are the moments life is made of and you will need to reflect back on this time and know you did your very best, that you made a difference to me in my final days. You did. You made all the difference in everything for me.

When there's a piece of your heart in Heaven, there's always a piece of Heaven in your heart.

PREPARING FOR THE PASSAGE

I didn't want to leave her but I was obedient first and foremost. I knew I had to go Home. She was sending me...and I was being called.
Reflections, Chapter 65

You've taken the first step. You've made THE DECISION. You've scheduled THE APPOINTMENT with the vet. It's on the calendar in black and white. It's real. No matter how much time we have, you are now well aware that our time together is fleeting at best. You want to spend as much time with me as possible.

When humans get very old and frail, they are lucky if they have a doctor who, as he orders up hospice comfort care for them, takes away all restrictions. Do the same for me because you will be glad later that you did. Looking back, you've given me everything! You gave me so much that I never wanted for anything I didn't have. Now it's time to really spoil me rotten!

Let me sleep on the bed with you. Give me all the ice cream and cookies that I want. Diabetes is no longer a fear for me. Nothing is really. There isn't any time left for that. Some hamburger from the dinner table would be lovely, the table you never fed me from because you are such a good master. Let me rest or let me play. Let me dig holes in the dirt or stay outside later than I normally would. A special trip to say goodbye to our friends at the park, a final farewell to our favorite beach, one last lounge on the front lawn. I'm probably not up for too many trips, but you know best. You can ask me and you will know by the wag in my tail or the absence of it – or the look in my eye or the tweak in my ear if that's one of the things I want to do. Mostly I just want to be with you. If you can take a day or two off from work that would be so wonderful for me and for you too. Whatever I want, please do it for me because it will all mean more than you realize when I am gone from your sight.

This is my time. I am well aware of what is happening because you told me, your heart to mine. It makes me happy that I am finally going Home and that I have your blessings in doing so. It's hard to leave you but I knew all along this would happen. I knew from the day we met. I also know that I will be seeing you again in time that will pass in the blink of an eye. Please promise me that you'll try to stay focused on the times we shared when life was good; when you never paid a second thought that it would come to this.

Some people delay and cling because they can't let go. Don't make me wait too long. I'm ready anytime. When all is said and done, more people feel they waited too long than those who felt they let go too soon. Our vet will help you to determine the best time and the best way. Don't forget to talk with me along the way and let me know what is happening so I can be better prepared too.

34

If you beg me not to leave, it will be painful for me because there is a complex mix of energies taking place. The physical body itself continues in its determination to live. It has never done anything else. It wants to keep living so it works against death. There is also an unseen and commanding but loving force that pulls me to the other side. All of a sudden I feel the force of you asking me not to go. Not to leave you. You don't need to say anything for me to feel this for I can read your thoughts. While I know I must go, I will still choose to suffer any amount of pain in order to be obedient to you. I am caught betwixt and between and yet my passing is inevitable. This is why it is important for you to give me permission to go for if you do not, you will look back and feel guilty for causing me the pain of your resistance. I don't want you to feel guilty because you aren't. Yet your potential anguish is so much worse and more painful than my temporary physical pain could ever be.

Kate would often look tentatively at my older sheltie sister Grady when she was sleeping to see if she was still breathing. Every night. Every morning. Naptimes. She would brace herself, hoping...fearing... Perhaps like you, Kate didn't want to have to make any decisions. She just wanted Grady go to sleep on her own and not wake up. She waited while Grady declined more and more. It was a very passive technique because Kate didn't want to make the wrong decision so she made no decision at all.

That which you avoid will keep coming back to you in order to heal whatever is getting in the way of your growth. Sometimes decision-making is a part of a person's growth. Kate always avoided making decisions that impacted others in her life. So here was Grady, her teacher, giving her the opportunity to step up to the plate. It's another gift, the gift of growth. The way I see it, you really can't make a wrong decision if you take the judgment out of it.

Kate had been waiting for God to call for Grady who suffered year after year, but God just didn't call for Grady. After awhile she got to thinking that maybe this was just a test of her love. Maybe it was a test to see if she loved Grady enough to let her go.
Reflections, Chapter 19

You've scheduled THE APPOINTMENT, but wait! I'm having a really good day! I am so active that it makes you question whether you are doing the right thing. It can be very confusing and may put you into a sort of agony as you proceed to second-guess your decision. Please don't cancel the appointment. It is just that I know. I know it is the Last Hurrah in this life of mine and I want to make the most of it! It is easy for me to have more energy because I am so happy about all of this. I'm so relieved. I know I am going Home soon where I will be free of pain and limitation. In the meantime I will purr and wag my tail and run around as best I can to show you how happy I am that I have shared this life with you and how blessed I am that you are the one I love! It's my final Swan Song. This is how I want you to remember me. I do not want you to remember me as anything but happy.

"THE APPOINTMENT"
EUTHANASIA

There are not enough words in the English language to describe the experience of this. Death is more than life. Humans put their animals "to sleep" when it's really waking them up. Everybody has it all backwards.
Reflections, Chapter 68

It is the most unselfish act in all of life to let one go that we have found beloved.

You don't want to think about it but it's the first thing on your mind. You say, "We made THE APPOINTMENT." You avoid the word "euthanasia" because it makes everything too real. It is a beautiful word, really. It is Greek for "easy death" and it is true, there is no easier death than this. It is unfortunate that, once again, people are so afraid of death in all its forms that they find it so difficult even when the time of death is peaceful.

So many say they put their pets 'down' when they are really lifting them up. It's true. Nobody likes to be put down. 'Putting To Sleep' is a much better term even though it's still not very accurate. Nonetheless, whatever words you use to describe it, you are helping me. Don't question your

37

decision again. It's the most loving thing you can do, to help me on my way Home.

To best be prepared, be sure to ask our vet to describe to you what you can expect. Find out what our options are – if it can take place at home or at the clinic. The right vet will calmly reassure us and accommodate our preferences and comfort levels. Kate had Grady put to sleep in our car under a shady tree outside the vet clinic. Grady always got very anxious about going to the clinic but she loved being in the car; she had spent so much time there making miles of memories. Our vet didn't make house calls at the time but more and more vets do now so that we don't have to be overly anxious or afraid. They make it possible to have an easy transition from the comfort of our very own bed. We can just close our eyes at home and open them in our heavenly Home. It's so perfect.

It is very important for me for everything to go as smoothly as possible during the appointment. Be sure that you are comfortable with the procedure and the cost that you and our vet have agreed upon. Hopefully our regular vet will be available because s/he is a familiar friend to me and it helps to know that s/he loves me too. I hope that the trusted staff will support you in your grief when I am gone.

If you can, plan on being there at the appointment with me and staying with me until it's done. It will not take long. If you need to bring someone with you for emotional support, don't hesitate to ask someone you love and trust to be there with you. Maybe it's even someone who loves me too, someone I would love to have beside us in my final moments. I was always the one who was there for you, so knowing that someone is with you at this time will reassure me too. You may also need someone to drive you home because you don't know what your state of mind will be later. How you handle this last visit is very personal and you must do what is best for you and for me.

The most important thing to remember is to help to create an environment for me as calm as can be under the circumstances. Being surrounded by love always alleviates pain and suffering. When we love and feel loved we are more immune to feeling the effects of physical or emotional discomfort. Love is a powerful force. My love for you and yours for me will get us through this appointment.

On the other hand, if you are crying and carrying on, it will make things more difficult for me and it might be best for you not to be present. You know how it always upset me when you were upset. Our final moments on earth impact the entry into our next life and it is always best if these moments can be as comforting as possible. If you are as calm as you can be and can just stay in your feeling of love for me, I can handle any tears that might come. It's your love I need to feel. Try to stay in the love and not in the fear. Really BE with me in the final moments. Like I taught you.

If you ultimately choose not to be present, I understand. Give me your love before they close the door and if you can it would be nice if you could spend some time afterwards with me, for closure for yourself and for me. If you cannot bear that, I understand. I am not in the body on the blanket on the table anyway. I am already on my way across the bridge to Heaven.

> *Do not stand at my grave and weep,*
> *I am not there; I do not sleep.*
> *I am a thousand winds that blow,*
> *I am the diamond glints on snow,*
> *I am the sun on ripened grain,*
> *I am the gentle autumn rain.*
> *When you awaken in the morning's hush*
> *I am the swift uplifting rush*
> *Of quiet birds in circling flight.*
> *I am the soft star-shine at night.*
> *Do not stand at my grave and cry,*
> *I am not there; I did not die.*
>
> *~Mary Elizabeth Frye*

The surgery I required put Kate between a rock and a hard place.

"If he dies on the table it could be blessing," she said, "He could comfortably just fade away." I would like to clarify that whether one is "put under" for surgery or "put under" for euthanasia, there is no pain. It is a most gentle transition. It's just that after surgery we are brought back and in euthanasia we are allowed to go.

I didn't die on the table. It wasn't supposed to be that easy for her. We still had more to do together. The most important part of our life together would come during the week that followed. I was blessed that I could die at home with her by my side. Death is the final stage of growth and she learned more in those last five days than she had learned in all our years together. Her love for me reached to the sky and would change the way she would come to look at everything. Had it happened any other way, any other time, you would not be reading this book or any of the others.

I had to suffer, for had I not she'd be clinging to me even now, wanting me to stay with her. It hurts when someone won't let go. Not only must we leave, we must tear ourselves from one who clings. My suffering served a purpose. She desperately wanted me to stay but her anguish in the final hours changed everything. It became her greatest desire for me to be free of pain and this ultimately made it easier for her to let me go.

Some of us need to suffer so that we seek relief, to be free from our own suffering. Otherwise we would never ever leave your side! In death there is much more going on than meets the eye. It's a fine balance of many things. Each piece of the puzzle needs to fit so all the other kazillions of pieces in the universe will fit too. All of us are connected all the time. Even in death we are living out our destinies together. All of our lives fit together like giant puzzle pieces. It's mostly about being in the right place at the right time. We are all continually connected to countless other souls who need us to fulfill our destiny...and a soul must stay on schedule.

Suddenly time stands still.
You. Me. The vet. The room.
...An IV infusion and in just a few moments a drop of my heavy head and in that moment peace comes at last. That long, well-deserved sleep after a hard day's work. When it is over and all is stillness, all pain and suffering are gone. It is

done. I am already at peace and my new journey has begun.

Remember when you would come home from work after a long and difficult day? You were tired already when the day began and you thought that it would never end. But it did. You cross the threshold and drop into bed and fall into a deep refreshing sleep. Later upon waking you feel so rested and relaxed that you don't want to move. You don't want to spoil the moment. You don't want to wake up just yet. That's what it's like for me. It's been a long road and even though I love you very much, I am tired. I am asking you to let me sleep now.

You have done the most thoughtful and humane thing for me possible. You gave me the final act of love. You set your own desires aside to honor what was best for me. You allowed me to run free over the Rainbow Bridge into a wonderful world where there is no pain or discomfort of any kind. It is a world that we will share together in a day that will pass when the time is right.

Please realize that my suffering was short-lived compared to the life I lived and loved with you. All of that life is but a blink of an eye when compared to the eternal life I am living now. It was just a tiny moment in time. You'll see when we are back together again. You'll see how it all works and you will look back and say how foolish you were to worry so. But worry, it's the human condition. It cannot be helped.

"Why?" You demand, "Why did he have to suffer?" "He never did anything to hurt anyone!" "He didn't deserve this!" The fact is: it is not for you to judge or decide. Keep in mind that death itself is not painful – on the contrary -- although the illness or injury preceding it might be. Death is just death. Death is a letting go and there is no better feeling once you are ready.

If I had pain or suffering, there must have been a good reason. Pain is a messenger; it tells you that it's time for change. It pushes you until you have no choice but to address it. You forget that there is a power over all things with the final say in everything. The fact is: there IS a reason for everything. Even for the suffering of an innocent being. Sometimes the only positive thing you have to hold onto is the relief in the fact that I suffer no more.

It's true. I suffer no more yet you continue to suffer the memory of my suffering. I am waiting for you to heal from this. Can you remember how heartsick you felt when you witnessed my suffering? It's the same for me. I don't want to see you suffer either! I am waiting for you to let go of the suffering...the suffering that no longer exists except in your own mind.

I really wanted to stay with her but my heavenly Master's voice is strong. I knew then why I had to suffer. The older we get, the more reasons God gives us to seek His comfort. In the end He sends us just enough pain and suffering so that we will want to leave. If everything were perfect, we would never choose to go. He wants us to seek an end to our suffering because He wants us to want to come Home.

Reflections, Chapter 63

AFTERSHOCKS

The overwhelming crisis has passed. I am now gone from your sight. You start to find that it really wasn't as bad as you were thinking it might be and yet you feel so empty. It's a strange time. You're probably exhausted. The hardest part of loss is the anticipation of it. Remember how I said fear doesn't exist in the moment? You are actually feeling better now that it's over. In this moment you feel relief that I am no longer suffering. You are also in a state of shock; you can't really access your feelings.

Soon you find a little more energy and what do you do with it? You probably start thinking too much again. Your thinking leads to worry and then you start questioning everything. It's a delayed reaction. You think your heart is broken. *"I'll never get over this,"* you say. You can hardly speak for the pressure of the sorrow that has come upon you. I know. When it came time for me to leave you, it felt to you like I had taken your love away with me. You think your love went with me but it did not. Feel it now. Feel the love you have for me. It is there, isn't it? It is there inside your heart. It is there because it is YOURS. It is your love for me. Because it is yours, no one can ever take it away from you. It is your love for me and mine for you that hold us together like glue through everything, through good times and bad, through life and through death. When you love without condition, your spirits can never be separated. The love you gave each other holds you together far beyond this life.

After I am gone you might look for all kinds of things to feel guilty about. Be prepared at this point for your guilt may be magnified, blown out of proportion.

"OMG, I killed my cat/dog/horse!" Or someone carelessly suggests that you did because you made the decision to end my earthly life. You did not kill me. If you did anything, you saved me. It was the most unselfish act you could have done for me, to escort me to the freedom that was waiting for me. You loved me enough to let me go. You freed me from being bound to a life that no longer served me. The truest form of love is where you are able to put your own needs aside to do what is best for the one you love.

While you continue to suffer, I have already moved far beyond suffering. You fear that I still suffer but I suffer no more. The moment I leave my body all pain melts away. There is no pain without a body! There are no nerve endings. There are no endings! The physical scars and painful feelings disappear as my final heartbeat merges into the rainbows on my pathway of peace. If you could know where I am now and if you love me as you say you do, you would never ever wish me back from the comfort of where I am and where I wait for you.

Still you deliberate. *What didn't I do? What should I have done? What should I have said?* You

46

torment yourself. *Did I wait too long? Did we do it too soon?* You did not wait too long. You did not do it too soon. This all comes back to your illusion of control. The fact is that there is a higher power that dictates the moment we will die. Each one of us will die when we are supposed to. Not a moment later, not a moment sooner. This is why some pets and some people seem like they are ready to die but they keep on living and others who appear to be very much alive are gone in the blink of an eye. There are stories of how certain pets were euthanized and yet it took some time for them to pass when it "should" have happened quickly. It is upsetting, oh yes, but they could only go when it was time for them to go.

I am sure that if anyone could have changed the outcome it was she but no matter how healthy the food was that we ate, no matter how many times my teeth were cleaned, there is an inevitable time and place at which point there is nothing in your power that you can do to change the outcome. In a certain time and place you will simply go in your own way.
Reflections, Chapter 75

"*Did he know I loved him?*" Of course I knew you loved me. See, you are already forgetting, putting me in the past tense, but don't go feeling guilty about that. It's natural until you learn what you need to learn.

Do I know you love me? The answer to this is the non-prescription drug that brings peace to everyone. Ahhhh to know we were loved! We all need to know we are loved and we need to know that those we love the most know that they are loved in return. Love is the drug. Love is the key. Love is the answer. Love is the question. Love is the secret. Love is everything!!! It doesn't matter what you did or didn't do. What you could have done or should've done. You cannot turn back the clock. You cannot change the circumstances. You never could change them. They were set in destiny, in the fate of the Rainbow Timetable. You need to love yourself as much as I love you and forgive yourself everything. You are not guilty of anything. You have loved me and love is always enough.

I know you can't think clearly. You are going through too much chaos in your mind and sorrow in your spirit to know what to do with all of this just now. The best thing you can do, now that you know that I know you love me, is to love yourself. Love yourself so much that there is no room for guilt, doubt or second-guessing. Love yourself unconditionally, the way I love you.

You think you are in control because you made a choice for me but you really had no control over much of anything. So often human beings try to maneuver and manipulate things to control an outcome but eventually most of them learn that no matter how focused and determined they may be, they cannot control much of anything at all. They are not supposed to control things because they are not in control! Humans can be slow learners and most of them keep trying to control stuff anyway just because it comes natural to them to think they can. Control is an illusion too. When you finally learn that you can go with the flow without feeling so responsible for things that aren't under your control anyway, it gets a little easier to have faith and to accept whatever comes your way.

Maybe you never had a chance to say goodbye to me. Maybe something took me quickly. When something immediate and unexpected happens, it can happen so fast that we end up at Rainbow Bridge and we hardly know what hit us. We are actually taken just before the moment of impact or trauma; experts have proven it. It is Heaven's way to protect us from the pain. This happens with people too.

Perhaps I died at the side of the road or maybe I was staying overnight in a kennel at the hospital. You fear that I was alone or that I felt alone but I did not feel alone. I was not alone. We are never alone. The closer we get to death, you cannot see it, but the more angels and guides surround us with their sweet embrace and welcome.

Maybe I crossed over while you were at work that day. You feel so much guilt that you weren't there for me, but I planned it that way. Please don't be mad at me. If I passed in your absence it was because I did not want you to see me in my final moments. I wanted to protect you from seeing me, from having those memories branded in your mind. I am very sensitive to you. I don't want you to see me until peace comes to my face...and the peace comes very quickly. If it had been meant to be another way, it would have unfolded another way. It happened just the way it was supposed to happen. It's how I wanted it.

Dogs usually find a private place and time to die alone. We don't want our loved ones to remember

49

us in our dying moments. But there you are on the
floor and there she is beside you and you cannot
move. You cannot hide. So I made the best of things.
Reflections, Chapter 65

One of Kate's friends had a beloved cocker spaniel. It had become quite old and was declining rapidly. The friend took the whole week off from work to be with her dog. She refused to leave his side the entire week, determined that he would not die alone. At about 10:30 one night, she stepped away from him just long enough to go the bathroom. When she came back, she found him. He had passed in the few moments that she had left his side. He was waiting for her to leave so he could leave the way he wanted to and needed to. People often tend to do the same thing. There they are, in their final earthly hours, their family surrounding them in a 24-hour vigil. The moment the last family member leaves the room for a moment, the person has the space to breathe their last breath in private peace. Not all of them -- but many -- do this.

Cats are quite famous for just walking away when the time comes. If they are old or sick, they plan their getaway and they do it with humble confidence and dignity. They value dignity above all. They have no fear.

So rest assured. Be pleased for me that I was able to do things on my own terms to the last second. Please don't worry for another moment! Don't you see that I did not want to say goodbye. Why would I? It's not goodbye!

THE PROCESS of GRIEF

Have you ever walked along a beach? You walk towards something in the distance. For the longest while it never seems to get any closer even though you are walking and walking. Then all of a sudden, you are there. You've arrived at last. That's what the process of grief is like. Meanwhile we are running along the edge of the surf with you and we are cheering you on.

It is morning. You are coming awake. For a brief moment you have a strange peace as you awaken from the In Between of sleep and awareness. Then it hits. Hard. You are jolted back to reality as it dawns on you what has happened and you respond, "Oh No. No No." (Denial) Your heart sinks. You feel fuel in your stomach that is uncomfortable and you are increasingly upset (Anger) that you can't turn back the clock and bring me back (Bargaining). Then you realize that it is of no use to fight it and you cry (Depression). You want to go back to sleep to escape the reality of it. Then you realize you must work today. You have no choice. You must do what you must do. (Acceptance).

For some this experience happens daily for a short time, for others who have more difficulty working through the loss it may take days or weeks. But over and over, every day upon waking, you work through the denial, the anger, the bargaining, the depression and the acceptance and eventually you will once again reach a place of peace and hope when you wake to a new day. This is like a little mini-course that keeps running you through the stages of grief. It's all preparing you for the work you have ahead of you. The day you wake with peace is the day you know you'll get through the rest of it. It's a day I will celebrate with you.

If you were physically sick you would go easy on yourself. You would have no other choice. Grief is no different. For a while you must take bereavement leave or sick time, withdraw from your social and professional obligations so that you have the space to heal and do what you must do to take care of yourself until you feel better.

You can only go one step at a time, one day at a time. It may feel like you aren't making progress or that it might actually be getting worse, but you are traveling two steps forward, one step back, not the other way around. You slip back but still you are further ahead than you were when you took the last step. There will be ups and downs throughout the process. Sometimes the ups will feel like downs. It can be most confusing because one moment you actually are feeling pretty good but in the next moment it seems worse than ever. There are reasons for this dynamic and this is normal. It is all by design.

As you progress you will find yourself changing. It's all very vague for you right now. You will feel your emotions shift and you find that you feel better simply because you feel different. It's like shifting positions after sitting in one place for too long. It may not necessarily be more comfortable, but it feels better because it's just different. You feel relief that your emotions have shifted for a little while until you feel that that doesn't feel too good either.

You might get weary from me saying It's All By Design but all of it is. There are no shortcuts. Grief is your teacher and you are the student and there is nothing else between you. The dealing with grief cannot be bypassed. It is a road you must walk, a race you must finish and no one else can do it for you. If you try to sneak through it without it seeing you, it will seep into your life when you least expect it. Grief will not let you go until you satisfy what it came to teach you.

As you retreat into the private world of your grief the material things of life around you tend to lose their meaning. All that matters to you is me. You wonder how you will ever live fully again without me. You'd give everything, do anything, just to have me back. At a certain point early in the process for just a moment you might see the truth. That your inner world (the world where I now live) is the "real" world while the outside world fades in comparison. Do you see, already grief is leading you into the moment, into yourself, into the heart of your soul? For a short time this is all that exists for you. The world that you think you live in revolves and spins around the world that is you. While the earth spins around the sun and the moon goes around the earth, they all spin around you. YOU are the universe. You are the center of everything. I have known this all along about you, for my world has revolved around you too.

Even if you have lived your life in service to others, putting your own needs last, this is the time for you to see that you are the most important person in your life. You have no choice but to look at yourself, deal with your loss, get to know yourself on a deeper level. You are being stripped to the core of everything you ever believed about yourself, about me, about life, about death.

WAKING FROM THE DREAM

*Life goes on and something is always turning into
something else. I now know this for sure:
Love is all there is and love never dies.
Love is energy and energy does not die; it cannot
die. Einstein would tell you that it is a proven
scientific fact. If it's energy, it must live,
although sometimes it changes form.
Love does not sleep. I am not dead. I am awake.*

Reflections, Chapter 67

It is an interesting experience when you are
getting ready to move from a place you have come
to love. When you know you will soon to be leaving
this world, every day is extra special and every
moment is precious. Everything that's been a big
part of your life you look at now, intently hoping to
never forget. You take it all in and on the final day
you hold it close to your heart. You know you'll
never ever forget this place as you move into the
next. You know beyond a doubt that you will never
forget your earthly home and the arms of the ones
you have held so dear. You. I will never forget you.
And I know. I know you will never forget me.

Like moving from one house to another, when
you leave you look back for a little while and it
persistently tugs at your heartstrings. You pull

yourself away so you can move forward and lo and behold you find that you have quickly adjusted to your new world, your new life. Even if you didn't really want to go in the first place.

Life leads to death, death leads to life. All dogs go to Heaven. All cats. All horses. All animals ("Animus," Latin for breath, soul, spirit, vital force). All humans. All spiritual beings. Each one of us exists far beyond the limitations and death of our bodies. This love will never end. How you handle my exit from this life will continue to impact our relationship going forward. Eventually we will all be reunited in the heaven that is our Home. We don't have to earn our way into Heaven, nor do you. We all enter Heaven when we are ready. We are all loved and we will all be together again someday. The laws of religion did not design this; it is universal natural law. We are all connected and love never dies.

"Oh no," they say. "Dogs don't have souls."
Or they say, "Dogs have souls but cats don't."
Where do they come up with this stuff? If something breathes, it has a soul. Breath is divine life force that comes and goes like the tides. This breath infuses every creature on the earth, in the sky and of the sea. It is evidence of the very spirit in every one of us. If it bleeds it has a soul, whether it is a man, an animal or a tree that gives its sap to the syrup.
Reflections, Chapter 78

As French philosopher Pierre Teilhard de Chardin once said: "We are not human beings living a spiritual experience, we are spiritual beings living a human experience." We are not so different, you and I. We are not just animals, you are not just humans. We are all spiritual beings, we are all teachers, we are all students and the earth is just a school where we learn important lessons before we go back Home.

We tried to make a heaven of earth,
But the earth is just a stage, a school,
Where we wear our masks and play our roles
And teach each other how to love.
Reflections, Chapter 85

An important thing you must come to realize is that there is an unlimited world beyond the world you think you live in. A world where there is no death, there is only a shift in life to something else. Change and loss and death and endings and beginnings, comings and goings and comings – they are all just a matter of time. It's the way of the world you live in.

You never went to New York City but you've heard of it. Even though you've never been there you know that it surely exists. You've heard people speak of it and you know of people who have gone and come back. Where I am is really not much different. If you got on a plane and went to New York you would disembark on the other side into a different world. The world as you knew it would disappear for a while until it's time to go back. When you return you find it is still very much there, just the way it was when you left it.

John Lennon said that death is like getting out of one car and into another, much like the well-known timeless poem, which follows:

Death is nothing at all. It does not count.
I have only slipped away into the next room.
Nothing has happened.
Everything remains exactly as it was.
I am I, and you are you, and the old life
That we lived so fondly together is untouched,
unchanged.
Whatever we were to each other, we are still.
Call me by the old familiar name.
Speak of me in the easy tone,
which you always used with me.
Put no difference into your tone.
Wear no forced air of solemnity or sorrow.
Laugh as we always laughed
At the little jokes that we enjoyed together.
Play, smile, think of me, pray for me.
Let my name be ever the household word
that it always was.
Let it be spoken without an effort,
without the ghost of a shadow upon it.
Life means all that it ever meant.
It is the same as it ever was.
There is absolute and unbroken continuity.
What is this death but a negligible accident?
Why should I be out of mind because I am out of
sight?
I am but waiting for you, for an interval,
Somewhere very near, just round the corner.
All is well. Nothing is hurt; nothing is lost.
One brief moment and all will be as it was before.
How we shall laugh at the trouble of parting
when we meet again!

Henry Scott Holland

SHOCK/DENIAL

*Oh my friend it is my first day without you. I forgot
for just a moment. I thought you were still here.
Later I got to thinking that maybe someone just
started a silly rumor and that it's all just a big joke,
but then I realized it's my denial. I don't want to
believe that you're gone.*

You are stunned. You're in shock. Denial. It's the
first stage of grief. It's by design because the
numbness protects you from feeling the full force
of your despair. Denial is a protective shield that
buffers you from your most troublesome feelings,
which will be unveiled to you little by little in small
doses over time so that you can better handle
them. You don't yet know or even believe that you
will heal from your loss of me. You haven't gotten
that far and you are even denying that.

At first you might be surprised that you feel
better than you thought you would. That's
because you aren't "feeling" much of anything yet.
Throughout this phase your emotions remain
submerged, hidden away until you are ready to
start feeling them again. It is the body's way of
healing itself, by protecting you from the full

59

awareness of the hurt, the pain, the suffering, the change and the devastating loss.

"You're gone," you say "and I feel dead inside." You feel this way because you're numb. I am not gone and you cannot be dead inside because I live on inside your heart. You don't believe this yet because you think when someone dies that they are dead. So you think I am just a memory that lives within your head.

You'll get through this. You'll find that I am very much alive and well, that our memories will never die and that I will help you work through the grief and find the love in your heart again. When you work through the denial you will feel again. You will feel alive, for better or for worse. When the time comes, you'll feel me. You'll feel me there. I will help you heal. I will help you feel. But I know you feel kind of dead yourself right now, suspended somewhere between death and life. It's shock. It's part of the process.

If you've ever experienced a great physical trauma, you know that you can go into shock as a survival tactic. You can be rendered unconscious or even comatose because the body and mind need to "shut down" so the body can be free to focus solely on the healing. The mind when it is in this non-thinking state is on a type of autopilot. It is temporarily "disabled." It's kind of how you are at this stage of grief. You have been traumatized. You are numb. All you know is that you are overwhelmed and exhausted and you don't have energy left to be thinking or doing anything more than getting through what you absolutely must do in your daily routine.

This is a time of hibernation for many. You retreat from the world at large whenever possible while your energy is increasing momentum in the quiet space of your healing. Deep within you are building a spiritual strength that is by design and beyond your control. It's your healing taking shape.

Little by little the shock wears off and you'll feel more of the pain. Little by little you must return to the world of family, work and social situations. Little by little you must step outside of your comfort zone. You will have unique challenges to face.

"Hey how's your dog doing?"

"He.... He died." Such a cold and hollow sound.

"He died." Isn't there another way to say it?

"He's dead."

"He did not survive."

"He didn't make it...."

These are some of the most difficult words to be uttered aloud. It's because by saying something you make it real. It feels like a lie because you are still in denial. You are answering the person's question, but sometimes you need to answer the question to be able to hear yourself speak the truth. It's these daily challenges that will help you to slowly move through the first stage of grief.

It is natural to replay all the details. Memories of me will run through your mind like a movie montage. You are starting to feel your feelings again and you begin to cry at the happy memories and cringe at the memories of my last days.

Deep in your heart you know what is true. Your mouth speaks the words, "My cat has died," but you still don't really want to believe it. You still find yourself going over and over and over it in your mind. Your heart replays the final scene for you for the express purpose of teaching you to accept what has happened. While your heart tries to "rewire" your mind to accept it, your mind keeps looking for a different answer. It doesn't like the truth. It wants a different outcome. Like anything else, when you hear it enough, you finally have to accept that it is true.

It's normal when you are this upset. The images in your head can be relentless. I was with you for an important part of your life. You don't know how you will ever learn to live without me but you will. You will learn to live in a whole new way and you will use the strengths that you have learned by loving and being loved by me.

ASHES AND MEMORIALS

She took great comfort in holding me. She was holding me in her arms again although she knew perfectly well that I was not In There. The ashes were all she had left of my body but memories of me were everywhere. We had gone everywhere together. Still she clung to that plastic urn of ashes.

Reflections, Chapter 72

There are still decisions that must be made. You probably have guessed by now that it's by design to keep your mind busy. It brings you back in touch with the tangible things of life. It's an important time as there is so much that you otherwise cannot touch and cannot feel and cannot see of me.

Perhaps you will bury me in the garden at home. Maybe you'll have me cremated and when you pick up my ashes you will speak the twilight zone-ish words, "He's back home." Back home in an urn on the altar or upon the hearth. Or perhaps you'll scatter my ashes on a favorite trail, in our dragonfly stream or in the nearby field where flowers dance. It doesn't really matter to me what choice you make because I want you to do what's best for you. It's what you do with your heart that matters the most. I am not in that hole in the ground. I am not in that urn full of ashes.

You are under a lot of stress. Please take plenty of time to think things through before you make your final arrangements. Consider the long-term possibilities. You must be comfortable if you ever move from the home where my body is buried. If you do move, please do me a favor; don't dig me up as some people do. I am not there. Let what is left of my earthly shell rest in peace.

Scatter my ashes or keep them, whatever is best for you. But if you keep them, please don't cling to them. It is the spirit in which you keep them that makes me happy...or sad...for you and for me. The most important thing is that you are comfortable with the choices that you have made for me. If you are going to remember me, remember me at my best. If you must think about me now, remember me with joy. It's how I lived my life. Remember the way I looked at you when death never entered our minds.

Do not make an altar of my final days or of my pain. Instead, create a treasure box of memories only for my life and the happiness with which I lived it. For the many loves that I had while I was there. There were so many! There was so much everything!

The design of the universe is vast and so is the array of creative memorial options. There are many factors that come into play and so many options to choose from when you wish to memorialize me. There are so many choices it can be overwhelming, but it gives you something to do for yourself in honor of me when you need comfort and care. You don't have to spend a lot of money.

If you can live in the moment, you can do everything with clear intention and make it effective for your healing.

One of the simplest things to do is to light a candle for me. Make a date with me; I will meet you there. Focus on the light and my life. Tea lights are safe and inexpensive. You might put one in a lovely candleholder to create a gentle glow in the darkness of your grief. Be careful however not to create another attachment. If you light a candle every night for me, it becomes another routine that you will one day have to break free from. After all, you would have to light a candle every night for the rest of your life. If you happen to miss one night, you might be filled with guilt and shame and blame that you did not remember to light that candle for me. Losing an attachment, even to something like this, becomes yet another loss. If your life is not complete without the shrine you made for me then you still have me on that leash around my neck. You are still not free, nor am I.

Please don't let go of your love for me, goodness no. Let go of the grief. The need. Learn this as you move forward. The less you cling to something, the less fear you have of losing that something or someone. The less fear you have, the more love you have. It is true that you love even more when you let go of the need for it. Love grows when grief goes. Make your love stronger than your fear. Strive to make your love greater than your need and let love be the most powerful force in your life. Then nothing can overcome you.

You may wish to set up a memorial altar – for my urn, my photo, memorial gifts and cards, my paw print, flowers, collars, tags. Set it up to honor my life, not my death. Celebrate my "Rainbow Birthday" not as the day I died but as the day I was born again. It is cause for celebration for on our rebirth in Heaven we do not come in crying like we do on earth; we come in laughing.

Maybe you will want to make a financial donation in memory of me to a pet-related organization or other charitable group that you wish to support. Donate my personal belongings to a rescue group or animal shelter. It would make me happy to have them used by someone who needs them, rather than storing them in a closet or on a shelf. One of the most personal things is the collar I wore every day. If you took it off of me and still have it, you can donate it to a friend whose dog is outgrowing its puppy collar. Or keep it. Or give it to Goodwill, the Charity Shop or Humane Society store. When I outgrew my first puppy collar, Kate found a nice green collar at the Goodwill to replace it. We always loved that soft faded green collar. I wore it for the rest of my life and we always thanked the dog who had worn it before.

Sometimes carrying something subtle and tangible with you helps to defer anxiety and nervous energy. Put my ID tag on your keychain. You can use it as a comfort stone when you are nervous about something. It can be a reminder during potentially stressful situations that I am there with you. This way you can carry me everywhere and nobody needs to know how you still need to feel me there. It keeps it between you and me.

You must do whatever feels right to you when you feel the time is right for you to do something.

There is no hurry. There are no rules. Do we have a garden? Did I love spending time there? Set up an area just for me where you can plant a tree, a rosebush or spread my ashes. Then be sure to observe the space because it is the perfect stage for me to send you signs and messengers!

We learned of a lady who got very ill after eating all of her husband's ashes. She is not the only one who has done this! I see you are making a face right now, but never judge another's journey. She was desperate to keep him as part of her. She obviously did not believe or have the faith that he would always be a part of her whether she eats him or not. There are healthier ways to keep my ashes close to you. You can hire an artisan to put them into a piece of jewelry or blend them into a polished crystal. Some will integrate the ashes into a custom tattoo. There are many ways to honor me, ways unique to you and me.

Some communities have pet cemeteries and special events with support for the bereaved. You can have a tree planted in my memory at a local park or hang chimes at a special pet memorial site. Go to our favorite dog park, say hi to our old friends and offer to donate a memorial plaque, a park bench or a tree that gives shade. Give something that will forever honor me and remind of your generosity.

Maybe our veterinarian had the thoughtful foresight to have an imprint of my paw made for you. Such treasured gifts are most welcome right now! Buy yourself something nice in my memory. Whatever suits you. You can even buy a star in the sky and name it after me! I'm Sirius! Consider having a scarf made of my woven hair. Have a photo canvas made of me or hire an artist to paint my portrait. A little angel coin or a worry stone that feels really good to you can be kept in your pocket to touch whenever you need to feel tangibly connected to me. Just try not to cling because in the event you lose that stone, that angel, it becomes another loss to grieve for it is an extension of me that you were hanging onto.

Sometimes one must be careful not to become dependent on "things" because something can be lost forever seemingly beyond reason, because you were too attached to it. By the losing of it you must then deal with the force of grief in its entirety without the crutch you created for yourself with that sentimental item which you have lost. Grief is designed to help you to learn to stand on your own two feet again...standing without crutches on the legs of your faith.

When you feel up to it, assemble our photos and create a space where you can immerse yourself in my eyes, my fur, and the world that we shared, whenever you wish. Begin to replace the unpleasant memories with memories of better times together.

The tangibles can help you when you are lonely and I am gone from your sight. This way, when you long to touch me, you can touch something that connects you to me through the power of our memory. It's just nice to have something – a stuffed animal, my blanket. You can even find plush animals that you can store my ashes in. Felted animals can be designed to look like me.

A creative project can also be therapeutic. Make a quilt out of my bandanas. Write a poem.

Paint a picture. Create a scrapbook or a collage of our memories. Telling or showing the story about me can be very cathartic and can serve as a memorial tribute that lasts forever. You can also do what Kate did and write something from your pet's perspective, perhaps a letter written from me to you so that you know how much you are loved! Be careful however, for if you tell the story too many times over and over, it can become a habit to the point that you don't know who you are without our story. It only compounds the loss. It makes it one more thing for you to lose: your identity as One Who Grieves. Balance is the key to everything.

When you have learned from something that has brought pain and suffering, when you discover the good that can come of it, you might want to do something that makes a difference to others who are going through the same thing. Some of the greatest works of art, music and literature are the result of deep love and great loss.

TEARS AND FEARS

*I have studied her tears through the years.
The human body was designed for joy. It can't
contain such sorrow. The heartache leaks out
through the eyes and sometimes through the nose.
Tears must fall for if they did not, the person would
be marooned on an island of sadness forever. Tears
flush the heartache away so the person can grow
and love again.*

Reflections, Chapter 73

You take a deep breath and summon your courage. You long to connect with me. You pull out the old photo album but you're not sure you can see me this way. The old cell phone with photos of the good old days waits for you to be brave enough to fall into the memories that we shared. I, too, wait for you to be brave enough. Meanwhile you are bracing yourself. Anxiety builds inside in the place where the butterflies rage when you're nervous and scared.

You may fear viewing a photo or video taken when we were vibrant and alive together. Maybe you fear reading a book designed to heal your grief, a book that will bring you understanding and permanent relief. You fear you'll never heal.

71

You fear you will heal. There is a fear of the truth and of the tears that will fall but each tear that falls holds potential for your growth.

If you can bring yourself to look at that photo, feel your feelings, speak my name, read that book, embrace what we had, tell me you love me enough to set me free...your courage to love through this phase will overcome everything and the fear will leave.

But you aren't ready yet. You are still on the edge of the denial of my passing and you are not ready to admit or believe that I am really gone. You think if you cry that it will be like admitting I am dead and gone. It's all just so complicated for you right now.

In your fast paced and modern technological age, it seems that self-discipline and control are valued more than genuine depths of emotion. In most future world sci-fi movies, people often look and act alike. They are cookie cutter, Spock-like – all brains and no emotion. What a dull world this world would be without the emotional qualities that make it come alive!

Some may view tears as a sign of weakness but only people who are strong will reveal their tears to someone else. There is no laughter without tears. There is no shade from the sun without shadows and clouds. There is no rainbow without a mixture of sun and rain. I will give you everything I can to help you move through this process so that you can be happy again. It's not any different than it ever was: I am not happy unless you are happy.

Remember when you used to call my name? It was like music to my ears. Even now it brings me back to you. It always will. When you call me I will come. You cannot begin to heal until you speak my name. I have a healing process too and because my heart is connected to yours, my healing is impacted by your progress or lack thereof. Until you are able to call me by name, you are stuck in denial, trying to pretend that not only am I not gone but that I perhaps never even existed.

You cannot begin to heal until you speak my name. Try it now. Right here right now as you read these words. Before you think too much. Say my name aloud. For me. I want to hear you say it and you need to say it too. For you. Speak my name and then share our story with someone you know and trust. Perhaps someone who even loved me too or who will come to love me because you do. It is in the telling of our story that sets us both free. You are stronger than your fears and you need to shed the tears. You cannot avoid looking at me for the rest of your life simply because I am here and you are there. We have loved each other! How can you not bring your eyes to meet mine, if only in a photo? Reminders of when we were young and vibrant, life was unfolding before us --- oh we had so much ahead of us! Now, how can you not open your heart to remembering this?

You allow your pain and your sorrow to take away the joy of remembering the good times. A memory comes up and you brace yourself. What will it be? Something that makes you cry? So what if it makes you cry? Why do you judge your tears? That's another lie that someone told you. That tears are bad. That tears are a sign of weakness. Tears are a sign of life and love and like the spring

73

rains that wash away the harshness of winter they nourish and clear the way for regeneration. Tears are a part of life. Sadness and sorrow are a part of life. Are you willing to cut off the life we shared together simply because you do not want to feel your sorrow or the wet tears upon your face?

I know how you feel right now. Our hearts are connected and I always know how you feel. I can feel you becoming irritated by all these questions. I'm sorry I keep asking you Why Why Why. Why, of course you have no answers for me. I want you to heal but you are not yet ready. I know you love me but I also know that you are getting tired of all these questions.

ANGER

She wanted to blame someone, anyone,
for her pain and her loss. Why do people feel better
when they blame someone? I don't know. Maybe it
just feels better to be angry than to be sad...

Reflections, Chapter 75

Most people don't want to go out for a while because it just takes a lot of energy to go back out into the big world. Those who grieve have little energy. Also when you venture out of the house again, there is the cruel reminder that life still goes on around you even though you grieve. It's hard to accept that life goes on for everyone else while yours seems at a standstill.

When you start shedding tears and feeling your feelings you are entering the next stage of the grief process. So far your denial has been protecting you by keeping you numb but new life stirs within. You are starting to "come to". You are entering a new stage. It is a time of frustration. Restlessness. Insecurity. Anger begins to rear its head and ultimately you feel worse because now you can FEEL you feelings. You realize after feeling dead for so long that you are alive after all and that you must go on living.

Anger can be misleading and misunderstood. You have witnessed what anger does to people. Angry people seem strong and powerful but things are not always what they seem. They really aren't powerful at all. They are presenting themselves as powerful to hide the fear and insecurity that inspires and drives their anger. Anger is always based in fear. It is a weak and defensive response to a real or imagined threat. Anger is like putting on a flaming suit of armor to protect oneself from something or someone.

Until now all your thoughts have been directed to your loss of me and your fears of facing your life without me. Now there is a surprising new energy that comes. It is an energy that is fueled by your anger. The fog of shock and denial are wearing off. You bring your mind back from its sabbatical and you might surprise yourself, maybe even scare yourself, with the powerful feelings of anger that may surface. You point your finger. You begin to blame everyone, anyone. Me. God. The vet. Yourself.

There's an important reason for the anger. Anger is energy and anger fuels you when you have suffered long and hard and your reserves are running low. For better or for worse it gives you power when you have little left. You have felt weak and confused for so long. You maybe have even wanted to die too, but now you are feeling stronger. Signs of life are emerging from within. Your strength is returning. You feel the power of your life force again. It is anger in the works.

The thing to be cautious about at this point and what you need to understand is that during grief you can feel hopeless. Anger is a dynamic point in grief. Anger is directly related to fear. Fear is directly related to hopelessness and despair. As you make your way into the anger and you feel your energy coming back, it can fuel your fear and your hopelessness and this is where some people will sadly take their lives. If only they knew that this was a passing stage and that they would be feeling better soon! But they did not have the information that you now have to equip themselves with the knowledge that would have prevented their own loss of life. This is beyond important and we will be discussing it in a future chapter.

Suddenly you are charged up and on a mission. Like Shock and Denial, most of this is not conscious it's just the way it is. You look around for a target. You will find your anger's victim somewhere for when you seek you will find. It's bad enough that you are grieving for me but now it's time to defer the sadness and desperation of your loss as your critical mind devotes its attention to seeking revenge. You've had a taste of your own strength and now you decide you would rather feel the fuel of anger. Especially if you feel the circumstances surrounding your loss could have been avoided in some way.

Easily angered by the events that have taken place, your mind becomes focused, fiercely scrutinizing each and every detail. Perhaps the guy who ran over your cat never stopped. Maybe he knew he hit your cat, maybe he didn't. You still find him guilty. And your father! Your father who left the gate open! Your dog would not have been anywhere near the road otherwise. What about that neighbor you now bitterly resent whose young pup went after your pet rabbit in your own front yard. Maybe the pup knew what it was doing; maybe it didn't. Maybe it was a prey-driven breed. Maybe it thought your rabbit was just another toy to play with. You rule the dog guilty and the woman too. And what about the local authorities? They did nothing at all about it! What good are they? And God. God! How could He let this happen? Humans have free will but God is always a handy one to blame because He is the one who sits on the throne. He is the one who allows or does not allow things to happen. He will gladly take the blame because He knows that someday you will understand and forgive everything.

You are now seeing all things through the lens of the anger of grief. If you are premeditating anything, if you have a plan for revenge, you must seek professional help to shift your thoughts away from it. This stage, while intense, is fleeting. It won't last. It's by design. You don't know this at the time because you can't yet see the forest for the trees. You don't need revenge. You need to work through your grief.

Still you keep revisiting the scene of the crime. You seethe when you think of the man, the insensitive vet, the woman and her killer dog, your thoughtless and incompetent father. You have thought of reporting them, suing them, defaming them. You've even thought for a moment of killing them for what they did or didn't do. It is the nature of the human mind to seek repentance and justice. You might feel much better coming from this place of power after feeling weak and vulnerable for so long. Just remember: True power comes from the love in your heart, not the rationalizations and revenge in your head.

If you are angry it can be uncomfortable but this is how you know you are making progress. This stage will pass sooner than later. Feeling the anger is okay, for you can heal what you allow yourself to feel. Expressing it is okay as long as you do it the right way with the right people. In all phases of grief, whatever your emotional state, it's important to have a safe place to express yourself and to be honored and accepted.

Your anger may build up to uncomfortable levels. Sometimes you may need to take a pillow and scream into it or beat it with a tennis racket. Sit in the privacy of your car and cry and scream and rant and rave, just get it out. If you are an athlete go for an extra hard run. Get out into nature where you are supported by natural forces. Bike. Workout. Even if you aren't an athlete. Get the excess energy fueled by your anger out of your system. When you increase your blood flow and activity level you increase your endorphins, which are the body's innate natural antidepressants. These are antidepressants that have no copays and no side effects. Your body has a built-in pharmacy and it knows what you need when you need it.

Many people are not well versed in how to manage anger. Perhaps as a child you were taught to repress it and now you don't know how to be healthy when you express it. You will find any number of people to be angry with. Your vet whom you had come to love and trust, 'He killed my dog!' Your father who left the gate open that day. You can rage about these things. You want to rant and rave; you might think about retaliation. You are in the full-blown anger stage and it can bring out the beast in you. Make sure you don't say something you will forever regret because of the fuel of your temporary rage and grief. You can carry this grudge with you until the end of time and hold it against your father forever, destroying in a moment the present and future of your relationship that has taken a lifetime to build.

Some people will understand your anger but most will not because, once again, people are just not comfortable with it. It is best to try to breathe and pause before lashing out at someone. If you clearly cannot find someone to blame, you can hurt the ones you love. It is irrational because you aren't thinking clearly. It's kind of like you want someone else to hurt as much as you do...even if you must be the one to hurt them.

Feel the anger but count to ten before you speak. Express it in a letter or an email but don't send it yet. Sleep on it and then see how you feel in the morning. You may not feel you need to send it at all because you feel better just having released your feelings in the writing of it. Chances are you'll sleep better if you let off some of the steam. God knows you need a good night's sleep. Save the email you drafted and look at it another time. Things can look a lot different in the morning. Then again, maybe you'll still want to send it.

Kate was treated quite badly on the phone by an Animal Hospital during my demise. Others have shared how the receptionist or staff at the vet's clinic was rude or seemed uncaring. Keep in mind that you are supersensitive right now so you may be magnifying the issue. Either way, if this happens you can continue to stew and brew over it or you can take action. Send a note to the vet – thank them for the good care they gave us over the years. Then let him or her know that this was how you were treated. Admit that you might be overreacting but share how devastating it was at a time when you most needed kindness, understanding and compassion. Kate owns a business and she would want to know if someone who worked for her was clearly uncaring or unprofessional. It would probably make you feel better to write the letter too for sometimes we need to act on something to resolve it so that it doesn't keep aggravating us.

So, once you've sent it – or not sent it – start the path to recovery. Take a walk or a run to de-energize the emotions you are feeling. Enroll in a yoga class. Beat that pillow. Breathe. Meditate. Count to ten. Sleep on it. A security blanket and comfy clothes to soften the edges of anger. Bunny slippers. Comfort food. It's time to find comfort wherever you can.

You find out when all is said and done that the only things you can really control are your thoughts and your attitude. You can choose to see things half empty or half full. You can choose to live in the moment where anger and fear do not exist or you can choose to live in the regrets of yesterday or the concerns for tomorrow, which are ruled by fear and illusion. If you can remember what I taught you about living in the moment, you know where I am. You always know where to find me. Here. Now.

On October 2, 2006 a man armed with a gun entered a Lancaster PA school and shot ten Amish schoolgirls. It was a senseless crime and the reason I mention this to you here is that the community at large and the parents and families of the murdered children joined together to offer grace to the family of the murderer and forgiveness towards the killer. In a world that is dominated by discord and revenge, these people somehow found peace in their community and within their hearts. If these parents can find peace in the senseless murder of a child, you can find peace too. Forgiveness begins with you. You need to want to find peace. I've taught you to look for the love in your heart whenever things go wrong. Seek and you shall find it.

When someone loves someone this much, they forgive everything. They will not even be aware that forgiveness is needed because they see you as perfect in all that you are and in all that you do. They live their lives in total love for themselves and for you, so that nothing you do can hurt or harm them because their love is stronger than anything that can happen. This new kind of love wipes every slate clean and becomes the basis of a greater love that will grow and grow until it is bigger and stronger than anything that could ever threaten to destroy it.

The Lizard from Rainbow Bridge, Chapter 23

I wish you the courage one day to defy the crime that continues to overpower you. I wish for you the willingness to look it in the face and say "No More!" and let it go. I watch and wait for the day you stop letting it dictate your thoughts, your feelings, your life; the day you stop identifying yourself as my victim. The day you stop letting it be more important than your love for me. The love that is currently lost in the shuffle of your rage and bitterness for the events of your life that took me away from you. I wait for the day you focus on the time you shared with me, not the moment that changed everything for us. Don't let it change everything. Honor me by forgiving the circumstances. Honor me by letting go of your need to seek revenge. Something had to take me to Heaven. Something had to happen. I couldn't stay forever. I tried.

We are all forgiving. We have tried to get you to see things from our perspective. When we forgive we no longer see anything that isn't love. We put it all behind us. It's not like we don't remember because we do. We remember the ones who hurt us and things like brooms and folded up newspapers. But we don't hold a grudge. We know life is too short to live in fear. We live in love and we wish that you could forgive each other, living in love instead of fear too.

I love you and I want you to be open to all the joys that life can bring and not be held back by your fear. We live in the possibilities that exist far beyond a doubting mind that believes the harshness of the world is irreversible. We live in love. We live in the moment where the past does not matter. All that matters is now and how we are going to make the best of things as we move into the future. When the past does not matter there is nothing to forgive. Love lives in the now. Love lives in the moment. When you live in the now in love, love rules over everything else. It's how I lived my life with you and it's how I wish you could live your life because it makes for a beautiful life and you deserve a beautiful life.

NOTE: You must be careful not to make too many important life decisions in the months of grief, especially during the anger stage, because you cannot yet see clearly. If you err, err in favor of waiting rather than making a wrong decision and going from the frying pan of your anger into the fire.

COMPLICATED GRIEF

When I crossed the Rainbow Bridge in the wee hours of that morning, I would not have expected Kate's father to be crossing over the following afternoon. It was complex, for while she wept bitter tears for me, she also cried guilty tears for the fact that, while she loved her father a great deal, she simply had loved me more. Dealing with yet another loss interrupted her grieving process with me. The anger stage she was supposed to go through with me she applied to her father instead. Once she was done dealing with her grief over losing him, she would have to come back and finish the grieving that started with me.
Return from Rainbow Bridge, Chapter 14

Every death brings up all the unresolved emotions of all the other deaths you have experienced. If you have ever suffered a loss and did not deal with it, it will come back magnified in your response to the current one. Some people do not seem troubled by a loss at all. They seem to be so accepting of it. Be aware that it is not always an insensitivity that makes someone appear unaffected by the grief. Some people are naturals at pushing the grief away, deep down inside, so they don't have to feel it. People think if they don't think about it that it will eventually go away but repressed inhibited grief does not go away by itself. It lurks around in the dark corners of one's being until loss rears its head again. You cannot heal what you have not allowed yourself to feel.

Unresolved issues of loss are stored deep within your cellular memory. Each death will not only bring up unresolved loss but also unresolved rejection, abandonment and separation issues. Loss is the common theme. Extreme and unresolved loss can cause volatile behaviors. It may create, for example, an irrational and overly protective parent or partner. The people who carry such issues with them will often have seemingly unreasonable fears, worries and anxieties. Their grief can be so extreme and exaggerated that they can develop disabling mental health conditions over time. All of the unresolved events of their lives that have to do with issues of loss can compound one on top of the other and then blindside them full force when a similar issue arrives on the scene. Like the straw the breaks the camel's back, it just takes one more incident to add to the others and there is nothing to do but to watch it come tumbling down. They typically must go through a type of breakdown so that they have no choice but to finally get the help they need. They look through a filter of grief and fear all the time and it never lets them go until they deal with the root cause of it.

Unresolved grief is not the only kind of complicated grief. Grief gets beyond complicated when there is more than one loss to grieve at one time. You never believe it can be worse than you until you hear about the others. There may be some upsetting things for you in the next few

86

paragraphs so feel free to bypass them if you wish. Please accept my apologies, but it's all part of life.

There are horrifying stories of entire families and pets that were swept away by the storms of life to their deaths in one way or another. Accidents. Fires. Floods. Storms. This creates a most complex form of grief. There can be one solitary survivor who remains behind who must deal with the losses all at once. Except you cannot grieve them all at once. It is not possible. You must pick them one at a time. So whom do you choose to start with? Your husband? Your children? Your brother? The family dog? All of them died in the fire while you were out picking up the pizza for dinner. Oh and you lost your home too...and guess what? You'll survive and you will be willing to live and maybe love again one day after you've gone through your healing. Of course you will never be the same -- but you will be okay. You'll be a new you.

Helping people through loss brings up more stories than the heart can hold. Imagine how it was for the cat and dog that died of starvation at home. Their water dish, bone dry, they were found lying on the floor beside their owner who had died several weeks before, unbeknownst to anyone. Or the guy who lived in the RV Park who had a spat with his neighbor. He came home from work to find his RV engulfed in flames with his three dogs inside. The man who adopted the aggressive dog to give it a chance. They did well until two years later when, in a fit of canine rage, the dog attacked the man. The man who had rescued him and cared for him came within an inch of his life yet was still willing to forgive. The dog was ultimately ordered by authorities to be euthanized for aggression. The lady whose dog bit her, provoking her other dog to respond by killing the dog that bit her in an effort to protect her, then that dog was mandated to be euthanized for aggression. What about the young woman who lost all her pets, three dogs and two cats, and one of her young children too, in a house fire. The young cat that was stolen from its home. The family searched in vain until the cat somehow found its way back home only to die soon thereafter from the acid burns and other abuses suffered at the hands of someone who had stolen him with intent to torture him, someone still at large. Or the woman who saw her tiny pup carried off by the coyote and who heard the cries far into the night. One woman came home from work to find her house burglarized. There was blood everywhere. She followed the trail to her bathroom and found her murdered protection dog in the bathtub. The woman lived alone. The crime is still unsolved.

These are all true stories heard firsthand along the way. Add to these, tales of millions of pets who live through cancer treatments year after year or those who live long lives with painful conditions and debilitating diagnoses.

You may be somewhat traumatized now just thinking about these stories. You get a little taste of how difficult it would be to erase such memories from your mind if it happened to you. If you are reading this and you too have suffered an especially traumatic ending, you know all about it. Trauma always makes grief more complicated. If you have been in this position you will find that you will need to heal the memory of and your feelings about the actual trauma first...and then work through the grief later. The trauma is going to demand your attention. It's a whole different kind of grief. You may need professional help to work through it.

If you happened to be there at the moment of impact or shortly thereafter, the images of the final moments, raw, with no time to prepare or protect yourself can knock you for a loop for quite a long time. It's a version of Post Traumatic Stress and it will come back to haunt you. It flashes through your mind like a shock; literally it's an electrical charge through the brain as you rewind and relive it over and over again. The memory will stay with you forever but the emotions and reactions that surrounded it will fade over time.

It is especially hard to resolve the unresolved. Perhaps there's been a hit and run driver or a perpetrator who could not be found or held accountable. Perhaps your pet was lost and never found. This too remains unresolved in the criminal archives of your mind. We know a man whose young purebred German Shepherd was stolen years ago. To this day when he sees a black and tan with similar markings, he investigates. He wants to make sure it's not his dog and if it is, there's hell to pay! It remains unresolved in his heart and still he seeks. The last time he looked at a dog thinking that it might be his he realized that it had been 27 years since his dog went missing. He knew in his mind that it could not possibly be his dog and yet still he searches his heart and soul because he never knew what happened.

How blessed I was to die the way I did. I was able to die lying on my favorite blanket on our kitchen floor with her beside me in the middle of a rainy night. I planned it that way. I had her all to myself and all the while we were both surrounded by the love of Heaven. I did not die at the hands of an abuser or worse, suffer a life of abuse and neglect only to be cast aside without care never knowing I was loved. Thrown into a landfill or dropped off at a shelter when I was old and needed care the most. What if??? I know it doesn't seem possible to you right now, but do you know how lucky I am to have shared my life with you? Do you know how lucky you are too?

Things will happen in her life and in mine so that everything takes place at the right time and in the right place. Sometimes a tragedy must happen to keep a soul on schedule. This is the reason for things that seem to have no reason. This is why you cannot fathom things that make no sense. It is not karma. It is not payback. It is not settling any score. It is not to hurt you in this life. There is a much deeper purpose at stake. Perhaps I will get very sick. People wonder why cancer exists when it is just a clever method to teach people lessons about love and loss and it borrows time or steals it depending on the needs of Heaven. It is just a temporary vehicle to get us where we need to be. It calls us Home because something needs us there. We always leave the earth for a very good reason. Perhaps I will be hit by a car and it will all seem such a tragedy to those who love me upon the earth, but it will be the way I can return over the Rainbow Bridge so that I can be there at the right moment in time to greet her as she comes across.

Return from Rainbow Bridge, Chapter 58

BARGAINING

Once you begin to realize that you will never be happy again if you hold all that anger locked up inside of you, you start rationalizing all of it. It's what the human mind does best. Maybe this. Maybe that. The mind will work overtime to try to offset the sadness and the ongoing discomfort. Thinking too much gives the illusion that there is no room for anything else. You think you can block the fear, the sadness and the anger by filling the space with a bunch of clever thoughts instead. You hereby move into the Bargaining Stage.

The mind keeps you most preoccupied because usually when people are unhappy they would rather be thinking about something than nothing. They would rather think of anything apart from the cause of their sadness. The process becomes its own diversion. The thinking can become a problem because your mind can easily lead you astray. You would actually come up with much better answers and solutions if you could only quiet your mind.

Different people grieve differently and the process of going through the stages of grief can begin as soon as death becomes a reality. In Kate's case the bargaining began shortly after my surgery when she did not yet know if I would survive; when she feared I would not.

"Dear God," she pleaded, "If you just allow him to live a few more years I'll _____(fill in the blank)."

"Oh Jack if you get through this I promise we'll take more walks and I won't leave you at home for so many hours a day." And so on.

Bargaining is the last ditch effort to change what has happened, to negotiate some kind of miracle. Her pleas went unanswered and she ultimately was forced to deal with my passing. The bargaining continued long after I was gone from her sight. She would rewind her memory back to try to "find" the tumor. It was as if she believed that if she could find in her mind the cause of it, she could change the outcome.

Denial, Anger and Bargaining keep you focused on something other than your pain. These stages have kept you "safely" in your head and out of your raw emotions. The anger was a cover up for vulnerable feelings; you didn't want to feel weak. But now the feelings begin to come, and the sorrow, and all the sorrows you ever felt that you never dealt with. You seek a way out of feeling the sorrow and oh, how clever you are! You find a way. You find a way that will detain your healing for a little while longer.

You enter into a fight with yourself. You begin a battle between your heart and your head. Your heart is leading the way but your head keeps looking for different answers. It doesn't like what your heart is telling you. What I am telling you. Alas you keep getting the same answer; the scene always ends the same way. Every time you see it replaying, you say to yourself, "No. It cannot be true." Replay. Replay. "No." "No". Every time you argue, "No".

Some difficulty arises when you get stuck on the replays. It's like a record with a skip in it. Playing over and over again the same answer. When you say "No, no, no, no." enough, the day will come when saying "no" becomes a habit. The head and the heart become disconnected. When you disconnect from your heart, you disconnect from me. You get stuck in your head and you forget about your heart and what it knows to be true. You make what your head is saying stronger than what your heart is saying. You totally forget your heart as you relentlessly look for different answers in your head. Your head will lie to you to keep you from seeing the truth that your heart wants to reveal. You and me, we are heart to heart not heart to head. Until you get back into the wisdom of your heart, you will not be able to hear me, see me, feel me. More about this in a later chapter.

Much of this you aren't even conscious of. You just know you feel terrible, tired, lost and confused. It's because you have forgotten the power of your heart. You've allowed the "no's" in your head to win. Meanwhile I wait patiently for you to surrender to the truth. I wait for you because I love you and I believe in you. I know you're getting closer to healing all the time. I have faith in you. I know you can do this.

If you find yourself replaying the moments or searching endlessly for excuses, there is something you need to do to honor me and to comfort you. One of the hardest things to do is to discipline yourself to stop replaying the final hours, but you must. Treat those thoughts, those memories, like the unwanted visitors that they are. They are thieves who are stealing your potential for healing. They taint your memories of me. They put your fear first and get in the way of the love that connects us. You must tell them to stay outside or go away. Remember, fear and love cannot live in the same space. Default to the love. Tell those thoughts, "You are not welcome here!" If you can stay stronger than they are, they eventually will obey you and fade away.

Kate still had moments when her thoughts would go to our final hours together. Where once she would have been wracked with sobs and tears, she learned to master control over it. Kind of like a song that is playing on the radio, the first few notes would come and she would recognize that it was a song she did not really want to hear, so she changed the station to find a better song. If you change your thoughts to a better thought, it will become a habit and the healing of your grief is guaranteed once you know how to do this.

Return from Rainbow Bridge, Chapter 29

You can do it. You've done it before. Think of a memory in your life that you are no longer attached to. Something that was very painful for you. The end of a serious relationship. A painful physical condition that is now healed. You've had time to accept it and learn to live with it. You remember vividly the circumstances but you do not feel it anymore. "Was that really me?" you ask yourself. It is no longer painful (unless you start thinking too much about how painfully traumatic

94

it was for you which means there is still something in it that remains unresolved). In fact you may not feel anything at all about it. It's just something that happened to you once. That's what it's like for us in Heaven. There is no attachment at all to the pain or suffering or difficulties from our life on earth. There is only Love.

Rest assured, someday your good memories will replace the unhappy ones. It takes time and for a while longer you will replay the bad stuff because you are still learning to accept things.

Sooner or later you realize that there is no bargaining your way out of reality. You've tried everything. You've bargained your way to nowhere. You face the reality that the only thing you can do is surrender. You realize that it's just life and love and death. You can't change what has happened. You know that now. There is no one to hold responsible.

But wait. Maybe there is...

WHO TO BLAME

She turned on herself. "What more could I have done? What did I do wrong?" She felt that she had been responsible for my life and therefore must be responsible for my death as well. She reviewed over and over what she could've done, what she didn't do, what she should've done. As animals we are innocent until proven guilty yet people seem to feel guilty until proven innocent. Why do people do this? Where does all that guilt come from? Don't you see that we are all innocent? Every last one of us!

Reflections, Chapter 75

Your emotions have risen to the surface of your constant awareness. You have now come to realize that there is no one else to blame. Once you've let everyone else off the hook of your anger and you have bargained everything you have, everything you are or ever will be, you begin to look at what you did or didn't do. You start questioning what you could have done or should have done. Your mind is shifting again and in the space created by the shift, it begins to clear, making room to feel more feelings and think more thoughts.

As human minds are prone to do, your mind empties but instead of staying empty it just fills up again. What happens with most people when they let their mind fill up again? It gets filled with Blame. Shame. Guilt. Because there is no one else to blame, you blame yourself. "What if we'd waited and taken him to our regular vet? Maybe she wouldn't have screwed up the surgery!!" "If we never had to move to this stupid town we would have had better care!!" "If I'd only come home from work on time he might not have died!" "If we had only done this, then that...." "Oh look how awful I am! I've made such horrible decisions!!!!" And on and on it goes. Humans are known for being judgmental and they are hardest on themselves. Your own mind is your worst enemy. Meanwhile your heart waits patiently to guide you to a place of peace where there is no blame.

There is a type of guilt known as Survivor Guilt where you find that you will gladly step up to the plate to take the blame for circumstances beyond your control. A dynamic that often takes place is a resurgence of guilt feelings for living your life. Deep inside, if you have not healed, you might feel guilty that you are the one who is still alive.

"Why not me instead of you?" you ask. You announce proudly with tears falling, stinging you with the nettles of blame and remaining anger, that you love me so much that you would've traded places with me if only you could. You would have gladly taken a bullet to save me but where does that leave me? Without you? The devotion is honorable but, like Romeo and Juliet, some people just don't stop to think things through before heroically sacrificing themselves for us.

If you were thinking clearly, you would never ever wish that outcome for me. Your feelings of guilt are tainting everything. From my point of view the answer is really quite clear. You can keep on living and caring for yourself without me but I could never live and care for myself without you. You must live longer than me. It's the way it's designed. You knew this when you met me.

When you love someone no matter how much time you have it's never long enough. You seem to forget that the sun must set. You know perfectly well when we first met that I would not be with you long enough. Yet when the time comes you weep and cry and ask God "WHY?!" as if it were some kind of surprise. Why? Because love changes everything. Love is the surprise.

I hear you say to someone every day that I was your "everything" but really you were my everything. You had your family. Your friends. You had your work. You had your computer and Facebook. You had things to do in life separate from me. What did I have? I only had you. So who is whose Everything? Don't you see this is why God designed me to leave first? I had to leave you first because I wouldn't have anything left if you left me.

It's supposed to be this way. We need to cross the Bridge before you do so we can greet you when you get Here. We waited at home for you there; We wait at home for you Here It's just the way it is.
  Reflections, Chapter 57

There is a type of envy that can accompany grief. It is a jealous blaming of others who have not yet lost their pet. *"What do you know about how I feel?"* you say, *"Your pets are alive and well!"* You set your steady gaze upon their pet, which triggers powerful memories of me, and while you sit there staring you wonder why they still have their pet and why you don't have me.

It is just a matter of time. Everything is. Everyone will lose everyone, whether you leave first or they do.   Parents will lose children. Husbands will lose wives. Pets will lose owners. It's the luck of the draw, a roll of the dice. You're never prepared. Someday, sooner or later, you will pass from this life too. So will everyone you ever loved. People seem to think they will live forever, but look around. Do you see anyone living forever? No, because those who are living forever are on the other side where I now live and wait for you.

You feel guilt for so many things. You feel it even if you forget me for a moment. One day you throw your head back in laughter at something really funny and then you come screeching to a self-conscious halt, now crying because you forgot about me for just that moment. You feel ashamed that you thought anything could possibly be funny enough to make you laugh when I am dead but I see it as progress. You're moving forward. Oh it made me so happy to see you laughing, it made me laugh too! It's what I want for you. It's what I want for us. I know I've said it before but there is nothing for you to feel guilty about. Remember, you can't heal what you won't feel and guilt is just a feeling; it isn't real. So allow yourself to feel it and then feel the relief of letting it go. I mourn your sorrow but I celebrate your laughter and I celebrate your tears. I celebrate your healing because your healing is the key to my happiness too.

SUICIDE

"I want to cross the Rainbow Bridge too, to be with my babies!"

Perhaps a loved one has crossed the Bridge and you are longing to be with them. <u>You must live out your life on earth and learn the lessons you need to learn before you can cross the bridge too.</u> You must grow from your life and your love and your loss. It's one of the things I came here to teach you.

THIS IS VERY IMPORTANT

There is a point in deep grief where some people feel they cannot survive the loss but thank goodness most of them do. Some of them don't.

Remember earlier we talked about how there is a reason for everything? How there is a Grand Plan in everything on this earth? There is a reason I had to leave when I did and there is a reason you are still here. You still have something important to do. You still have life lessons to learn. You must heal and learn and grow in love and wisdom so that one day you too will easily be lifted into the vibration that is Heaven. Going with the flow of life is like catching a train at the station. You need to be at the right station at the right time and board the right train to get you where you need to be. If you go earlier than you're supposed to, you can catch the wrong train. You don't want to do that because it will just take you further away from me than you feel you already are. You need to go through the growing pains of grief so that you and I can fulfill our destiny and be in the right place at the right time to be reunited again.

You can regret that maybe you made a poor choice – life is full of poor choices that are designed to teach you -- but to shame oneself is one of the first padlocks on the freedom of the heart and soul. The roots of guilt and shame run deep. Guilt and shame are prevalent in our society and they are destructive forces. Guilt says, "I did something wrong." Shame says, "I am something wrong." These thoughts will bring everything crashing down for you when you are grieving. You will not just question the loss of me; you will question your own self-worth. You will start questioning this even more when you experience guilt and you ask, "Why you not me?"

If you are truly feeling hopeless and you cannot shake it, please call a local bereavement agency, hospice or clergyperson. If you have a friend or sponsor you can call when and if you need to talk, this would be a very good time to call them. If you are considering suicide and have a plan, contact 9-1-1 or a suicide hotline ASAP. Now. Put down this book and make the call.

In the US: 1-800-273-TALK (8255) or dial 911.
In the UK: dial 999 or 112 or 111 Option 2
or dial the National Emergency # in your country.

What you need to know is that hopelessness is a part of grief but you don't know that when it is happening to you. You don't see things clearly when you are blinded by your sorrow and your loss. When people are sad they tend to see only the dark side of things. When they are suicidal, they feel hopeless and can see No Way Out. IT IS A TEMPORARY STATE. Please don't give up. It is not who you are. It is what grief is. It is your nature to heal and you will. Not only that but you will come out of this much stronger than you were before for what you have learned.

If you try to come Here sooner than you are supposed to, you will disrupt The Divine Plan. Do not interfere with it. Your arrival here is predestined just as mine was. You can only cross the Rainbow Bridge when you have learned all the lessons you need to learn in your life on earth. The longer you live, the more you learn how to love. When you have learned to love (and be loved) enough, you will be granted admission. You won't need to do anything to make it happen. It will be decided for you by a loving force that knows what's best for you. Keep going with the flow with the knowledge that we are watching you, loving you and patiently waiting for you.

The ultimate tragedy is when someone has medical or mental health issues that have gone unaddressed, mismanaged or undiagnosed. Perhaps they have lived a lifetime of stress, struggle, strain and confusion, all on a foundation of shame and feeling to blame for not being "better" "happier" etc. They are ashamed that they are What They Are when the reality is that What They Are is sick, disabled or chemically imbalanced. They can't see things clearly and are unable to control their moods or impulses. They go through life at best wearing their Mona Lisa smile, often seeking nothing more than the long-awaited relief when their own death, sooner or later, finally comes to the horizon.

These are the premature and unnecessary deaths that could have been prevented. These are those who spend a long overwhelming life of struggle trying to be 'normal' while running against the wind, judging themselves and getting weaker with age for lack of faith. All the while they never knew that they were experiencing a physiological condition that could have been corrected. Some who have suffered longstanding abuse issues find that memories hidden even from their own awareness can come back to haunt them, triggered by new loss, grief and trauma. These unresolved issues can keep them from love and intimacy and ultimately guide them instead to invest their love in a safer relationship. They focus on loving and trusting their pets instead of people which prevents them from accessing the human parts of life that make the living of it so worthwhile.

She had made me her everything.
She didn't realize then that
When you make someone your everything,
When they are gone you have nothing left
...And after all, only God can be your Everything.
Return from Rainbow Bridge, Chapter 37

More suicides are taking place in the world today than ever before. The best revenge on deaths like this is to make up your mind from this moment forward to treat everyone and every living thing with respect, kindness and dignity. Including yourself. All the time. No one person is better than another. Some will look down on you for whatever subjective reason. Some will look up to you and then feel jealousy, envy, or even adoration. Later on they may surprise you by putting the "one-up" down to feel better about themselves. Not everyone is equipped to handle casual insults and shameful remarks. The ones that put on a happy face while internalizing the hateful comments are the ones who often will hurt themselves or someone else.

"But he was such a nice guy. I can't believe he'd do something like that!" "But she seemed like such a happy person."

Many school killings and bombings and other premeditated group murders have been committed by kids, young adults or adults who have been estranged, bullied and misunderstood. This is why it's so important to treat every human being with kindness and care. It's also why you should always be sure to nurture a few good human relationships so that you can support and be supportive of each other in times of crisis, celebration and grief.

It can be a fine line between life and death.

No one on earth can do it alone. This is the reason why she and I visited the sick, the dying and the infirmed. There were many of them who were loved, but there were some who had never known love. They were the ones we wanted. We wanted them to know that on this earth they were lovable and we showed them this by loving them. The whole point of life is to learn love. Life is the school love is the lesson and we are all here to teach each other to love and to be loved.
Reflections, Chapter 94

It can get complicated. The fact is that when you admit that you can't blame anyone or anything else, you begin to blame yourself. The human mind gives up trying to find an executioner but still it must blame someone. Anger that is not expressed tends to turn inward and will attack the very one who feels it. You move from anger and guilt into depression. It is a powerful time when your world seems empty. Believe it or not, it is a time of healing and transformation -- and pain. There is nothing to take your mind from it now. Not even your own mind.

DEPRESSION

The puppy mill lady glared at Kate and she was angry with me. "You need to show these dogs who is boss!" She pressed me harder and harder into the sidewalk on my back with her hands on my front legs like handcuffs. I could not escape! I tried for a little while but then I gave up because she was just stronger than I was. This is kind of how it is with grief and loss. You enter innocently into a situation. The situation challenges all that you have ever been. You fight, you flail, you do whatever you can to change it – to bring your loved one back – but all to no avail. You eventually realize that it is just a waste of your time and energy and you are forced to give up. You surrender to the circumstances. Like me pinned to the sidewalk, it wasn't until I stopped struggling and became obedient that I was allowed to rise up out of the situation.
Return from Rainbow Bridge, Chapter 32

You have no energy left. You've no desire to fight anymore. The battle is over. You feel you have lost but you have not lost. You are surrendering because you finally realize that the only way to win is to surrender. You have to admit that there is absolutely nothing you can do to bring me back.

There is also no one else to blame and nowhere to run from this life without me. You have been living in limbo while wallowing through the Twilight Zone of grief. Now you must find out who you are without me.

To outsiders, depression seems simply to be an emotional condition that may be flat, sad and/or apathetic. In reality unexpressed anger must go somewhere and its natural course is to turn inward, attacking the very one who feels it. Depression is your anger turned inward. It gives up the fight and it wears and tears on your own self-esteem. It can't shake the guilt. The residue of your own unresolved anger can attack you like a masochist.

Grief's fourth stage is a normal reaction to the stress of loss although sometimes it can trigger a medical or psychiatric emergency if it gets serious enough. Acute depression can come in response to the need to adjust to something painful and permanent. Healing is a fine line. Grief's depression is not something that needs to be "fixed." It arises from life circumstances that one must feel and express in order to grow.

It is very important to devote yourself to getting through this. If you have not resolved your grief, it will affect your future relationships including the one you have with yourself. Including the one you have with me. It will keep us all in a holding pattern, putting a straightjacket on your love and chaining you to the past instead of moving you forward into the future.

You are no more guilty than a child is guilty for his parents' divorce. You are no more to blame than the young girl abused by a sexual predator.

But look, even as children under terrific stress, these are their prevailing thoughts. They are ashamed. They feel to blame for not fighting, for not saying "no." They take the blame upon themselves for what someone else did. They take these shameful and unresolved thoughts with them far into adulthood to be repeatedly triggered by life events over the course of the rest of their lives.

Matters of life and death are out of your hands. The more you come to realize this, the harder you try to prove that you can control SOMETHING, anything. All you can really control is your response to what happens. You cannot control matters of life or death and because of this you are not accountable. You cannot be held liable for anything that you have no power over. Guilt, shame and blame make no sense when circumstances are beyond your control.
Return from Rainbow Bridge, Chapter 16

There is no guilt, no blame and no shame. They do not even exist. These are just illusions of the human mind. You believe in them because someone taught you that they are real but they are not. What a waste to spend one's life under these conditions. There is no freedom in a life filled with shame. There is only the continual ongoing need to feel "good enough" for something.

You are good enough! Do you remember how I looked at you? My eyes adored you! I saw you at your best; I witnessed you at your worst. I saw things no one else would ever see. I loved you inside and out and through it all I saw the truth of who you are. Why can't you see it too?

109

People who are depressed tend to isolate themselves. You've witnessed them, no doubt. Their homes reflect their depressed state of mind. They close the windows and draw the shades. They keep themselves in the dark. After a while it's almost like they have cobwebs growing on them. The cobwebs are their icky thoughts. When you stay in the dark long enough it can be hard to break free and to find your way out. It's like you're afraid you'll be blinded by the light of day.

Try to make a conscious effort to stay out of the dark places in your mind. There are so many of them. Most people who are grieving get stuck in their heads and they won't find much of anything good there. Always try to keep the focus on your heart and the love and light that radiates from there. In the heart there are no dark places. If you really want to heal you must pull open the heavy drapes from the windows of your mind and let the sunshine in.

It's especially difficult for people who live alone or who are disconnected from their families. Perhaps I was the only one who accompanied you through the difficult transitions of life. I saw you when no one else knew what you were going through. I know what you are capable of and I know you'll get through this too.

If you want to connect with me, it's best to get out of the confines of the house and into the vastness of nature. Breathe in some fresh air. If you live near a beach, put your feet in the sand. If you live near a park, put your toes in the grass. Sit with your back supported by the sturdy trunk of a tree. Connecting with nature will help strengthen your own roots. Go to a fun movie to escape from the grief for a little while. Read books that will raise your spirits and carry you into the vibration that is love and faith. You cannot see my signs and messages when your mind is in the dark. You must get out and moving. Get out of the house. Step into the light of day. Fine-tune your awareness and engage your senses again.

Each stage of growth involves loss and each stage involves pain. When you feel the pain of loss, please don't grab at something or someone to take your pain away from you. It's a human tendency when one is in pain to run away from the discomfort. You will tend to seek relief in whatever way possible but you cannot run away from this. You flee only to find yourself one day wishing you had never run away in the first place.

Be willing to feel the pain and have faith that pain, like everything else, is transitional. It is a teacher. Ask it what it has to teach you for on the other side of the pain you will learn something important about who you are.

This is a most delicate time. You might consider doing things you would not ordinarily do. You could become drug or alcohol addicted in order to find escape. You may even think of committing suicide because you feel you cannot get past the desperation of your loss. You feel like there is a hole in your heart where love seems to be missing and you try to fill it with a substitute for love.

There is no substitute for love. There is not enough drink or drug or comfort food or diversion that can take the place of love. Addictions, medications and other superficial diversions can only hurt you or divert you, in the long run. They numb and propel you backwards into your grief. You can only substitute love for love so the secret is to build up your faith and prepare to bring another kind of love into the space my love seemed to leave behind. Love for yourself. Love for another. Both. This is the strategic point where some will bring a new kind love into their lives.

Antidepressants and antianxiety drugs may dull the pain so that you don't feel it and they may be deemed necessary for the short term. Remember, what you don't feel you won't heal so if you are not planning on being on medications for the rest of your life, you will have to deal with the depression or loss at a later time. You will need to deal with it sooner or later. That said, if your pain is so bad that you simply don't know how you'll survive, you will need something. Be sure you have a doctor who understands you and can adjust dosages and taper you off when the time is right. Just remember, it is a NORMAL reaction to loss, feeling depressed. It's one of the stages of grief. It is a normal phase of adjustment to a loss in your life. It will pass if you just keep going, but if you don't feel you can keep going, seek medical or psychological advice and support.

Sometimes you can convince yourself that you have dealt with your loss and have been depressed "long enough" but even if you have worked through certain parts of the loss, you can find yourself in its depths again and again. Don't be afraid to confront your grief. Ask your depression and your grief: "What do you have to teach me?" We will give you an answer that will come into your thoughts, through your dreams, in the words of someone else...a messenger. One way or another we always find a way to answer you.

One day in a time that cannot be predicted you will have to admit that "Yes" it is true. What happened is true. I am gone from this earthly existence. I am not coming back in my particular physical form to this particular physical place. Once you truly comprehend and internalize this, you can move forward with acceptance in the deepest part of your open mind. As soon as grief teaches you what you need to learn, you can move on to the next stage and ultimately move out of the grief altogether, moving forward to live your life on new terms with the new understanding you have gained from your teachers: Grief. Me.

THERE IS NO DEATH

You now ask me where I am.
I'm with you! Where else exists?
There is no "other" place.
There is only one, this one.
I'm not somewhere out beyond the stars!

Do you think that Heaven's far from Earth?
It is not far. They are the same!
The place doesn't change; it's we who do.
The body that you think is "you",
Well, it isn't you at all.
It just contains and separates you
From the Heaven that surrounds.

One day you will leave it too,
Just the way that I left mine.
You'll be surprised but you will find
The moment when you shed your skin,
You'll see! We'll be together again.

Reflections, Chapter 85

"My pet lives at Rainbow Bridge," many say, but we don't really. Rainbow Bridge is exactly what it implies. It is a passageway between you and me. It's a full spectrum bridge that's made out of our love. I am on one side and you are on the other. The love between us is the bridge that connects us

115

forever. It's a bridge that takes us both to our ultimate destination. It's the entryway into the light and the love that is Heaven. It will open up to you too someday when the time is right. It will open up and span across the space between you and me when you too are ready and able to cross. Yet it is a space that holds no distance. The other side is as close as your next breath. It is all very abstract and hard to explain for there really are no words to describe how you cross the bridge but as you do the bridge gradually disappears behind you as you take each step, as you close the gap which actually holds no distance, and rejoin with me, soul to soul. It is my hope in the meantime that you will come to see that I am always with you. We don't have to wait for you to cross the rainbow to be together.

It might be difficult for you to comprehend because it is so different from what you may have been taught to believe. Can you believe...can you understand...can you fathom this truth? We all live in the same space. That includes you and me. Right here and right now. I know it's hard to believe if you've been taught that Heaven is up in the sky somewhere beyond the clouds. We all live in the same place. Heaven is all around you. You just can't see us most of the time because we are vibrating at a higher level than you are. It's kind of like a dog whistle. There is a noise, a pitch so high that the human ear cannot detect it, but it is there nonetheless for look, all the dogs come running! When I crossed Rainbow Bridge I became only love and love is the highest level of vibration possible; the highest "pitch" so to speak – and this is why you cannot see me. I am here, only gone from your

116

sight until one day you leave your body and become the same vibration that I am. In that moment we will be together again. When you vibrate in love all the time you will never again have to ask if I am here; you will know beyond a doubt that I am here with you.

Only gone from your sight...You and me, we can still share powerful moments of connection if you can keep quieting your mind, raising your vibration, tuning in to me. Tune in with all of your (six) senses, the senses that I use to communicate with you. Heal yourself by tearing down the wall of grief that you have built that keeps me apart from you.

You may find this hard to believe but our story does not end. Life does not end here. The end of this life is not the end of life at all. There are no words to describe how beautiful this is, this unique and overly feared experience of death and dying. If there were words in existence beautiful enough to describe Heaven, I would strive to find them so that you would never be afraid of it again.

The most important thing you can do for me is to not cling to memories of my sickness, my suffering, and my death. I am no longer sick. I no longer suffer. I am not dead! If you truly love me and if you knew the state of well being in which I now live, you would never wish me back from here.

The biggest problem is when you get desperate, needy, longing for me, crying for me, begging me to come back to you... then you bind me to you with your need for me. I am then suspended in limbo until you work through it. It's like keeping me on a leash when we are at a most

117

lush and wonderful park. While all the others run joyous and free, I can only stand and watch helplessly because you bind me to you in your grief. I know you don't mean to do it. It's not about cutting the leash of love that binds us. It's about cutting the leash of grief that tethers us to your sadness and holds both of us back from healing.

These are low vibration thoughts and when you are in that space, that energy, we cannot meet. Remember, fear and love cannot live in the same space and those thoughts of yours create a wall I cannot pass through.

No doubt you've heard of ghosts and spirits who are trapped in their old lives and who continue to "haunt" the earth by their being trapped. There are multitudes of lost souls suspended on the bridge between earthly existence and heaven, either because they weren't ready to leave — or because someone still clings to them, binding them to the earthly plane, unwilling to let them cross the bridge when they need to be free.

I am not the only one to stress the importance of letting go. Jesus said it. Buddha preached it. Singers from all eras have sung about it. William Shakespeare wrote of it. "Thus I let you go," says Anthony, "and give you to the gods." You complain that I have not made myself visible to you yet, but I cannot return from somewhere I have not yet arrived, can I?

"Mary, do not cling to me
for I have not yet returned to my Father"
(Jesus to Mary Magdalene upon her finding him
risen from the dead.)
John 20:17

118

Letting Go doesn't mean you don't love me anymore. Letting Go doesn't mean you won't miss me anymore. You can never cut the ties that bind two souls together who truly love each other. It's a fine line between clinging and letting go. In fact, it's not really letting me go, it's just letting me BE without clinging to me. When you keep your grief alive, you keep me dead within your head. Please work through your grief. Surrender to What Is so that I can live again. So that you can live again. I know it's hard. I had to learn to surrender too when I realized I only hurt myself by fighting what I couldn't change. I learned. It's one of the things you need to learn too so that life can be easier and so that death can be easier. Love is the lesson of life but so is the letting go. I learned early.

You need to heal for you and you need to heal for me too. I cannot be calm until you reach a state of calm too. Don't forget: We are connected by indestructible heart cords. Not only that, but I feel everything in my heart that you feel in yours. Soulmates truly live within each other and my home is still with you. Home is not where I live, home is where I love. I live in your heart so it is important if you care about me to care about yourself enough to heal for the both of us.

You created a comfortable home for us on earth. Now create a peaceful environment in your heart that makes it a pleasant place for me to be. Once you can see the forest for the trees you will know. There is no safer place for me. There is no way to be closer than we are right now.

When you remain attached to me,
You keep the chain around my neck.
Please free me from your leash of grief.
By doing so, you free yourself.
Remember how I was in life,
Always right beside you?
Always at your feet!
You did not have a leash on me.
There was no fence. I was not chained.
I stayed close by because I loved.
Don't ever question where I've gone or
Where I am when you can't see.
There's nowhere else I am and
There's nowhere else I'd rather be.

Reflections, Chapter 86

YOU CAN HEAL WHAT YOU FEEL

Cautiously she returned to the world at large. She really had no choice, for those who are living must go on living. Yet at the same time she felt that she did not want to progress. Not really. Still so attached and focused on me, she felt that if she continued to grieve it would keep me closer to her. While it's true that grief keeps us close, it also binds us together and keeps us locked in the grief when it's time to move on and live and love again.
Return from Rainbow Bridge, Chapter 22

It is the willingness to feel your feelings that heals you. It is the willingness to look life and death in the eye, knowing you are stronger than any of it. It honors me when you are willing to move past your grief to remember the wonderful times we shared. These are the times I want you to remember! You fear each tear that falls and yet each tear holds the secret to your growth.

If you can finally look at my photo and speak my name, embrace what we had and let the gentle smiles come through your tears, all fear will melt away and eventually all that will be left is love. It is what I'm waiting for. It's all I've ever wanted.

Some people cry for a little while. Some people cry for a very long time. Tears are an important release. If tears are not shed, they take up valuable space and block your ability to heal. You judge your tears when they fall. "Look at me," you say, "I'm still crying over you! Why? Why am I still crying over you?!" Why? It's because you've never had a love like mine. You'll never have a love quite like mine again. You cry remembering the hard times and you cry remembering the good times.

Finally the day comes and your tears are different. They are slow giant tears that take a long time to come out of your eyes and slide down your cheek. As you allow yourself to heal, the tears come slower and heavier. This is a sign that you are healing. They are full of the weight of your love for me and your willingness to shed them. They are sweet now where once they were bitter. There is no sting. The sweetness comes with time and surrender. These are the gentle tears of acceptance.

It's human nature to heal and you are doing it. You're getting ready to be free from all sadness and grief over me. The smiles will come. The tears will go. The first time you realize that you smiled without the tears is the beginning of becoming who I taught you to be.

The pain of grief can cause you to think too much and then you go into the fear and then you feel vulnerable and when you feel vulnerable you typically close up your heart at the most important time when it needs to stay open. Your heart is the door to my everything. If you close it off, it matters not how close we are. I am stuck on the other side of the door that your grief has

122

closed between us. No matter how I try, I cannot reach you. It's the love that joins us together, that keeps the door open; it's the love that creates the Rainbow Bridge that forever and always will connect you to me. To be able to see me you must unlock your mind and open your heart.

When you start feeling better and find yourself smiling or laughing, when you begin to feel happy again, please don't feel guilty about it. Don't turn right around and cry about it. It's a sign that you're healing and that's what I want most for you. I am watching for signs of your healing and I celebrate every time I witness them. When you find the joy in your life again I find the joy in mine as well. There is nothing better than joy that is shared, no matter what side of the rainbow we are on.

ACCEPTANCE

God grant me the serenity
to accept the things I cannot change;
the courage to change the things I can;
and the wisdom to know the difference.
~Reinhold Niebuhr

Acceptance can be misunderstood. It doesn't mean your life is perfect or that you think it is. You can still be missing me and crying heavy tears but you aren't fighting anymore. You have surrendered. You have admitted that what has happened cannot be changed. You've accepted the fact that your life will go on, with me or without me.

Only those who avoid love in their lives can avoid the pain of grief. Please don't let yourself be one of them. Those who avoid love probably learned to avoid it because of a previous experience of the pain of loss. It is a vicious cycle and it can become an obstacle to climb over if you are to live a life that is worth living. Love is what makes it worth living. It makes the world go round. It makes the ride worthwhile. I am the one who brings hope into your heart. I am the one who will bring you back to believing in love, inspiring you to be willing to take the risk to love again. The love is always stronger than the pain. The love you give and get is what gives you the strength to move not only through the pain of loss but through every challenging situation for the rest of your life if you learn what I came to teach you. If you learn what grief came to teach you. You will find looking back that you never lost anything at all. That I am still with you. That your faith will see you through everything that can happen and that in the end everything will be okay.

You suffer more by resisting and refusing to look at the truth than you would if you just let go and accept and let grief have its way with you. What you avoid in life will always come back. What you resist persists. What you allow yourself to feel will allow you to heal.

This is the stage where you will move from resisting to adapting. Of course you cannot go back to the way things were. You may never appreciate what happened but you will come to accept it. One piece of life at a time, you will learn to show up differently.

It takes some people longer than others but you will adjust. It is human nature to adapt to change and once you work through this final stage you may find that you need to incorporate new ways of doing things into your routine. You might have to find new ways to maintain your fitness if you are no longer hiking the trails with your dog. I don't know what Kate would have done without my Facebook Page. She made it for me as an album of my life and was going to close it up at my death. Her friends said, "No No! Keep Jack's page! We love him so!" So she adapted and began to share our journey of grief and then the book and well, the rest is history. This is an example of a big loss that turns into something bigger. Nothing is ever all good or all bad because something always comes out of something if you allow it.

You never do fully recover "You." You will never have another relationship exactly like the one we had. You will become more for the loss of me and you will move forward into a New You. The You I helped you to become. All you can do now is to begin to create the beautiful New You that has been born from your love and from your loss.

Whatever you decide is okay with me, as long as you make it a goal to heal your heart. Some people are determined to forever remain in the house that we shared because they want to keep things the same. After all, it holds many memories of our days together. Other people want to move and begin a clean slate and that's okay too. When you move you take all the memories with you when you go but you have a chance to live differently. You'll learn new things and meet new people. You'll learn to live in a new place and love a new home and create a new garden. Learning new ways of doing things can accelerate your healing. Let that new thing happen. When you wonder if I might see it, just remember that your heart is my home. I see it. I see it all. Know that wherever you go I am right there with you.

Life is short but life is long and sooner or later, whether you move or whether you don't, grief needs to be shaken to make room for new opportunities to help you to get to know the New You. After all, while you live upon the earth you must make the most of it. You must live your life as best you can. Living in endless grief is not living.

When you have healed you'll be more confident and you will find yourself willing to take some risks again. I can feel you saying now, "No, no, no. I don't want to take anymore risks..." You aren't quite ready but when the moment comes I want you to remember the risks you have taken that have made your life better. I want you to remember the risk that you took that very first day when you brought me into your home and your heart.

GROWING PAINS

I feel like I have lost myself. I want to find the "Me" that went away with you. The part of me that loved so unceasingly without condition. The part of me that loved the way you taught me how to love. The part of me that felt more real than I ever felt before. No one seems to find that "Me" and I can't find Me either.

There will be growing pains and much like having shoes too tight, it can be difficult to move forward. To shrink away from the experience of loss, to seek escape from the growth, will have dire consequence. One cannot escape destiny. You run with no particular destination in mind. You think that anywhere is better than this place. When you get there you find you keep running because you don't really want to be anywhere at all. Wherever you go, as they say, there you are.

Other kinds of losses may follow. They will reveal themselves in time. Loss of identity. Loss of a way of living. It is the loss of so many things rolled up into one package but mostly it is the loss of who you were before the loss took place that can take its toll on you. You don't know it yet, but it takes hold of you with the intention of lifting you up to a much higher place.

You have identified for so long with being mine. My best friend. My nurturer. My provider. My child. My parent. My partner. My everything. Sometimes when you love this much you forget that you can do it on your own. Suddenly you don't know who you are without me. Over time you might find that you grieve for so long that you don't know who you are without the grief. It is a natural inclination for you to then remain a victim when you see no way out.

Sometimes it seems to me that you would rather continue grieving than to feel the space in your heart and in your head, a space that exists only because there is now a vast room of potential that comes from your experience of a higher love with me.

You complain of 'the hole in your heart' but it isn't a hole in your heart at all. When I left you I took a piece of your heart with me. I filled up the hole with a piece of mine so that we would never ever be separated. Your heart feels empty to you because the love you felt for me was greater than any love you've ever yet known and your capacity to love grew and grew, much like the Grinch who came to his senses before Christmas was through. Your stretched heart is just waiting to open wide for you to work through the grief so that you can love again and be loved again, better than you ever loved before. Love grows when grieve goes. Believe it or not, it's what it's all about. It's all about the Love.

You say your heart is 'broken,' that I broke it when I left. It grieves me to think that I hurt you, but it simply can't be true. I came into your life to make you strong not to break you...and now my

Master nods approvingly and says, "Well done." Your heart is stronger than anything. You heart just feels broken because right now you associate me with the emotion of sadness, which makes me sad too. Someday you'll see that I made you stronger. Someday you will know that your heart is not broken at all. The heart can never break.

The day will come and you will kick off your bunny slippers and venture out of the safety and security of your home. You'll put on your "happy face" and join the world and interact again. And pretend to be normal. Sometimes it's true that you have to Fake It Till You Make It.

You may find yourself feeling incompetent. Your self-esteem can plummet because of the grief that has weighed you down. You're not sure who you are. You might feel insecure and vulnerable. You're different now. You're not quite who you were because you grew from losing me. Sometimes it's hard to know who you are until you see yourself from the eyes of others. Going back out into the world a step at a time teaches you little by little that you are still capable, still valuable, still wanted, still needed. You find you are still you. You are still loved. You are still alive.

Soon comes the learning of new things and growth. When our first book came out on Kindle, we offered it to our support group members for free. We gave simple step-by-step instructions on how to get it and how to read it. When you grieve it's hard to learn new ways of doing things so there was some resistance from those who had never read a digital book. A year or so later, we offered it for free again. Many people who had claimed to be 'technologically challenged' the year before, downloaded it this time and not only were they successful downloading it but they celebrated the fact that they had accomplished it!

Grieving is a learning experience. It forces you to grow in ways you have resisted growing before. Trying to learn new things when you grieve can be like running against the wind but when you have grown and found peace in the storm you have more ability to learn than you had before. Like running against the wind, it makes you stronger. You are wiser. You are moving forward.

As you grow and as time passes, no matter how much you love and miss me, you will find that you forget about me once in awhile. You will then feel the guilt that still comes so easily to you, but when you forget about me it's a really good sign -- because you once thought about me constantly for the longest time. It is a break for you and for me too. You'll find you have a good day here and there and then a few good days in a row and then maybe a week. You might slip back and have a bad one because there will always be good days and bad days. In due time the good ones will far outnumber the bad.

I know what you are thinking. You can't now fathom ever forgetting to think about me. You're afraid that if you move forward, it will take you further away from me. This is a common misconception shared by many people and it delays their healing while keeping us stuck on the Bridge. It keeps you stuck in you grief and it's only because you are still clinging to me. You think if you stop grieving that you will lose me. Maybe you even feel if you let go of me that you are abandoning me; maybe you feel that you will hurt my feelings because if it were the other way around you would not ever want me to forget about you. You are afraid that if you love again that you will grow away from me.

I am Here! I am here, waiting to run to you when the time comes. It's unconditional. It's forever. You can never lose me. Someday you will see that I was with you all along. You will find out that what you have loved you can never lose.

ANNIVERSARIES

Every grieving mother knows how old her child would be today. You know how old I would be now and how long I've been gone. The heart remembers everything. You are connected to me by the love that we share, a love that tugs at your heartstrings at special times. You might find yourself thinking about me continuously one day. You just can't get me out of your mind! Maybe you even have a dream of me or receive an extraordinary sign. You look at the calendar and realize that it is the anniversary of my passing or my gotcha day or my birthday. The heart remembers everything. I will not allow you to forget the celebrations of our shared life.

"One day without him..."
"He was still here this time last week."
"I've made it through the first two weeks."
"I can't believe she's been gone a month."
"It's been 2 months, 2 days, 7 hours, 35 minutes."
"3 months have passed now."
4 months."
"5 months...152 days"
"I'm coming up on 6 months."
"It's my first holiday alone."
"This would have been her birthday."

We've made it through one year of loss. We've been through one round of all the anniversaries of the heart. 365 days of "first times." Oh, but it's still complicated isn't it? Leaving the first year behind, it's like we lose that too.

The anniversaries will keep coming. There will be days when you just aren't feeling so strong. Maybe you go the park where we used to go and even though you have a new friend with you, you are filled with tears and memories of our days together. It's okay. Let them come. Those were the days my friend...

Creating new traditions is a very good way to move forward, to honor me and to honor the special days of the year. Sometimes you need to create new traditions for yourself when you are faced with loss---or if you are struggling with family issues and disappointments.

Anniversaries and holidays can be difficult at best when your life feels empty or incomplete. One of the things you can do for yourself during these times is to celebrate the life we shared. Do not mourn my loss. Celebrate my life. Create a lovely altar, light a candle. Say your prayers. Invite me to visit you. Talk to me. Tell me about your hopes and dreams. Reflect on the good times. Tell me you love me over and over again. Soak in the happy times of being blessed by someone in your life who loved you and who loves you still. Someone who taught you the meaning of love, not fear. Celebrate our love and know that love never dies.

When you are visiting people over the holidays who might not understand what you are going through, take something tangible and subtle with you; something that you can wear - or hold in your hand -- when you are feeling more connected to me than you can feel to them. It's okay to talk about it if it feels like the right thing to do for you. It's okay to not want to talk about too. Just tell them that. It can also be quite handy to excuse yourself so you can go to bed early. That's okay to a point too. You have a very good reason and you are learning at last to take care of yourself. Balance the holiday and try to stay balanced as you move forward to the next anniversary without me. Balance is the key to all healing. Time and support will take care of the rest.

If you want to avoid parties and dinners and celebrations altogether you can do what Kate did her first two holidays without her father and me. She volunteered at a soup kitchen. She knew that she would feel better helping people less fortunate than she. Over the Christmas holidays she visited her family. She traveled back across country on Christmas Day, leaving shortly after breakfast and the opening of gifts. She timed it this way so she would not be at home too long with family "celebrating" the joy of the season, four months after our crossing the Bridge. She occupied herself with travel because she did not feel joy at the time. When you are surrounded by joy it can actually make you feel worse when you feel worse.

The first of every month would loom ominously. She braced herself every time a new month approached. The August 1 anniversary was tough. Then a funny thing happened. December 1 arrived; sixteen months. The day came and went. On December 2 she realized she had not noticed. She felt guilty at first until she realized it was a sign of her healing. My life was the important thing and our relationship, now on new terms, was all that mattered. She forgot February 1 too! And March! She didn't remember until after a whole week had passed! Who knew what would happen on April Fool's Day? Well! She fooled me and remembered! This is how it will happen for you too, in your own time and in your own way.

Return from Rainbow Bridge, Chapter 62

THE LANGUAGE OF THE HEART

I speak silently but if you listen you can hear me.

People use the cliché, 'my head knows that you are gone but it forgot to tell my heart.' They actually have it backwards because the heart knows everything. The heart knows all truth because it looks at everything with the power of love. It hopes your head will catch up and know the truth: the truth that I am not gone at all. The truth that Love Never Dies.

Man will explore the galaxies of the universe and find ways to land on the moon but never think to explore the depths of his own heart. There's a big difference between the head and the heart. Fear lives in the head. Love lives in the heart. The head thinks it knows it all but the heart is always right. The heart is the most important thing. Some people don't even realize that a heart has a purpose other than beating and circulating blood through the body. It is much more than an anatomical part. It is the key to everything. I have experienced this firsthand, for the heartbeat is the first thing that brings us into this life and it is the last thing to leave. Our heart is the bridge that brings us here and it's the bridge that takes us back home.

If you can keep your focus on the love in your heart instead of the pain and fear in your head, you will feel the power that is there. You might even feel me there. Love and fear cannot coexist and if you focus on the love then you will feel your fear disappear. When you get the fear and the clinging out of it, that's when the magic happens.

Kate did not hear me for the longest time. I was very patient and very persistent, as all of us are, for love makes us so. It was at least six months after my passing when one night I finally broke through her wall of grief. I had worked so long so hard to get her to hear me and she finally did! It was so exciting for me! She wrote down what I told her and she has never stopped listening. She listens to me even now as she writes this book for you. She listens because I need her to tell you that I represent all souls on this side of Rainbow Bridge. We have all be trying to reach you and now that Kate can hear and translate into human words, we will speak to you through her. We will speak through my voice, which speaks to her through the power of the heart. Soon you too will learn to receive communications, our hearts to yours. It's just a matter of time.

There are certain expressions and experiences that need no language, no tradition, no religion or cultural structure to completely understand their meaning. If you were to look at photographs in a foreign magazine, a magazine written in a language that you don't understand, you will see the eyes, the smiles, the tears, and the sorrow. When you see these expressions there is no need for translation, no need for explanation. You feel those feelings in your own heart when you see them on the face and in the eyes of someone else. There IS no explanation for the there are no words to fully describe pure joy or desperate sorrow. It is joy and sorrow that will remind you that you all belong to each other and that you have more in common with each other than not. When you use limited language to explain such deep things, the words always tend to fall short.

One of the most important things I taught her during our life on earth was the language of the heart. I taught it to her so that we could communicate in our life together there and I taught it to her so she would ultimately be able to hear me speak to her heart from Here.

It is a language one does not just speak and hear, but a language that one can sense, feel and understand in the echoes of the spirit of their soul. The language of the heart is the true universal language. It's like déjà vu. The closest way I can describe it is like an old familiar song or a smile or a soulful look in the eye. It is the very language every heart speaks and understands, country-to-country, lifetime-to-lifetime.

It's not the words we understand when someone speaks to us. It's the energy behind them, the spirit in which they are said. I won't remember the words you said to me but I'll remember how what you said made me feel. The power of the tone and the force of the feeling behind your words is the key to the power of the heart.

The words that people speak are just a tiny portion of their communication. When you take away the voice, the speech, the words, there is still a great deal of expression taking place. Words are shaped in the limited mind. The desire to express comes from the heart. The heart is the true center of communication. When you speak from the power of the heart, the angels at all points of Heaven will hear you.

Be vigilant about the words you use and how you say them for they can create your reality. "I love him to death!" "It's killing me." "It makes me sick." "My heart is broken."

Like a distorted prayer these words and concepts driven by intense emotion radiate out into the universe where they begin to take shape. There is an actual condition called "Broken Heart Syndrome" that you can literally bring upon yourself if you remain stuck in your negative thoughts.

Are you still waiting for a "sign" from me? I am waiting too. Your refusal to heal affects me profoundly. I keep waiting and watching patiently for a sign from you. A sign of your healing. A moment of contentment in the storm. Some peace of mind and a smile that lights up your heart and makes it a happier place. I live with you, we all do. Everyone you ever loved with your heart and soul (notice I don't mention your head) lives within you. We are in your heart and we are here to stay, only gone from your sight. If you can quiet yourself and stop focusing on what you are thinking and focus instead on how you feel, you might be able to feel us there.

We await the happy day when you throw open the shades of grief, clear out the cobwebs of your negative thoughts, dust off the residue of guilt and blame and flood the entire place with the light of your healing and your love. Can you imagine how good that will feel? Like coming back to a warm and cozy home where someone loves you after being stranded alone in the bitter cold and blinding blizzard of your mind where you cannot see and are so numb you can no longer feel yourself. You seek only warmth and relief. Nothing more. Step out of your head ...and back into the home of your heart.

You are your own storm. You are your own relief. We all wait for you to turn on the warm light of your love again. It's your love that connects us. It's your fear that keeps us separate. The light of love and the shadow of fear cannot live together in the same space, just as darkness will disappear the moment you shine a light upon it. We are waiting for you to shine, for you and for us. It's up to you. Only you can turn on the love light in your heart that will reveal us to you. Only you. It's always up to you. Why do you choose to remain in the dark when you have a light available anytime you choose to use it? It's okay. We wait patiently. We believe in you and we believe in love over fear. Love always wins.

You may not realize it but you are communicating with us all the time through the thoughts that you think and the feelings that you express. No matter what side of the Rainbow Bridge we are on, my soul is your soul and your soul is mine. I watch you. I hear you. I feel you. I observe your body language. I see the world through your eyes. I watch your gestures and listen to your tone of voice.

Like words that sound the same but are opposite, sometimes I couldn't tell if she was laughing or crying. They kind of seemed the same. I would have to look very carefully at her eyes and her mouth. I assessed the tilt of her head and her breathing pattern. I got good at deciphering her, but sometimes even when she was laughing, tears would come out of her eyes. Humans are strange that way. They live such a dichotomy.

Reflections, Chapter 29

I have learned to understand you and even now you can learn to understand me too. I do not use words, but you must remember how I have communicated in other ways. You learned to understand me without my saying a word. I couldn't really smile but I could wag my tail. I couldn't speak my joy but I could jump and squirm and wiggle and whine when you came home from work to show you my joy and my love for you. You would get hot under the collar because you were angry and I got hot under the collar too. My hair might have gone up on the back of my neck or my head might've felt hot to the touch. See? There are many things you can understand through observing body language and mood. What is your body language telling me?

Most of all I spoke from the heart, my heart to yours. Most of all I loved you and I always will. It's all I want to think about. It's all I want to talk about. I am the one at the party that inspires everyone to roll their eyes at each other because all they hear about from me is YOU. That's what you do when you are consumed by love for someone. When you're in love you don't care what anyone thinks.

THE GIFT OF GRIEF

When you think back on your life, from whom have you learned the most? Was it the one who wanted to please you, who was easy to be with? Or was it the one who pushed your buttons, disappointed you and challenged you? The one who frustrated you to no end and you sometimes thought life would be better without them.

You can learn more in a moment from someone who challenges you than you can in a lifetime from someone who doesn't. Such is grief. It pushes, it disappoints, it challenges. Grief is your teacher. Grief shows you many things, including helping you to see what you will do differently next time. If you are wondering what you should have said or should have done, start saying it now. Say it to those who still live.

While your healing is inevitable, you are never truly separate from your grief. Because it is transformation on the deepest level, what you've learned is integrated into everything you are and everything you will come to do.

The personal experience of death and the gift of grief sensitizes you to all of life. It takes you into the depths. It shows you extremes. It brings you to the truth. It takes you deep into the foundation of your being where, like the plant that drives forth its deepest roots, you will grow into a spiritually stronger person. If you go deep enough, you can repair and make peace with the unrest that perhaps has been living for a lifetime in the roots of your heart. If you go deep enough there will be no wind strong enough to shake you. It takes courage but you are doing it already! I'm so proud of you.

Grief is a gift that will affect you in many ways as you move forward in your life. The day will come when you will stop and look at how you respond to something or someone. You will take pause. In a moment of spontaneous reflection as you observe your own behavior you will tilt your head to the side, perplexed, and say, "Is this me? Could it be?" Yes it is! It is the New You! You will be amazed at how healthy and wise you have become from all you learned from loving me and losing me.

Learning to live with loss makes you more real. More willing to feel. More authentic. More compassionate and sincere. More aware of the sincerity of the people around you. Also more perceptive of those who are not so sincere. There is a depth and wisdom you will possess because of the love we've shared. You will experience a preciousness of life because of what I helped you to become by loving you beyond love. This entire experience is moving you forward and deeper into a brilliant spiritual awareness and social discernment.

I caution you that stepping into this New You will likely change some of your relationships. You will be living at a much deeper level than some of the people you have had in your life. You may find yourself frustrated or bored by conversation that only skims the surface. You may need to find more depth in your life – in a group, with new friends, a new relationship or new pursuits.

It is interesting that once you have the space in your life from losing me, something or someone wonderful often can step into that space to be with the New You, the one who lives more deeply and with more love and faith than you've ever known before. The New You becomes a magnet that will attract a higher love: a new kind of friend, lover or opportunity.

Discernment is a gift of the soul. What about those needy friends who felt they needed you when you were not available during your time of grief? What happened when they came to you for help when you were suffering? Did they understand? Some did perhaps. Many probably did not. Are they there now to comfort and support you? No, many of them are nowhere to be found. So if you are lucky, they walked away from you while you were doing what you had to do for you. Don't spend another moment crying over it. They were doing the best they could and they did you a favor to show their lack of compassion and care for you. When you think about them now, do you not feel relief that they are gone?

Compare the way you feel about me to the way you feel about them. They are at the other end of the spectrum. They do not love. They have conditions for you or they would still be there by your side. Look at the ones who are still there. Look at them for they are the ones who love you without condition and without judgment. Now you know beyond a doubt who your true friends are.

I was also a gift. I was a gift of life and of grief. I was created just for you. As a lovely song goes that she used to sing to me, when God created me he was thinking about you. He was thinking about us. He knew what we both needed. I am a gift that has been given, not something that has been taken away. When you can appreciate what you have had more than what you have lost, you will find that you can apply it to all areas of your life. You have learned that you cannot experience happiness without sadness too because in this fleeting and bittersweet moment when you are happy and on top of the world, you know deep in your being that this moment is leaving. It simply cannot last. Everything is always turning into something else and soon it will be a memory. The fact is, if you can rise above the earthly realm and live without fear, you know for sure that love will always win. You have the faith that love never dies. You live in the moment because this moment is precious and you now know that this moment is all you really have.

DREAMS

THE MEETING PLACES OF THE SOUL
Reconnection -Reassurance –Reconciliation

I have found the way into her mind. When she sleeps her overactive brain is sleeping too. The mind takes over, taking her wherever her soul wants to go. Dreams are the meeting places of the soul. Sometimes I can even catch her just before she falls asleep or in the moments when she wakes."
Reflections, Chapter 95

"I wish the Rainbow Bridge had visiting hours." Another cliché. Well, it does! It's called the Land of Dreams and it's open all the time. When you dream your body stays in the bed but your spirit travels into the very same place where I am. Dreams reside in your soul, accessed by the heart where all wisdom lives, beyond the veil beyond the doorway of your heart. The eternal memory of everything lives in your soul not in your head. That's why the harder you use your brain to try to remember something deeply important the more it escapes you until you stop thinking about it. Your heart slips in through that tween time space and then "ding!" you remember it just like that.

Dreams are the meeting places of the soul. Dreams are where we meet with you to work through things. Dreamland is not far away and yet to you it seems like a foreign land. Guess what? There's a special language that we speak here. It's called the Language of the Heart! It's what I tried to teach you when I lived with you on earth. It's what I've been trying to teach you through your healing process. I always knew you would need it some day, when I would be gone from your sight.

Feelings, senses, metaphors and symbols are the universal language of dreams, signs and other afterlife communications. It's how we speak to you because we can't typically express through the spoken word. We never could. Once in awhile we can put you in a place where nearby people will find themselves suddenly inspired to speak the words we want you to hear--- or a book will fall off a shelf whose title is something we want to tell you. Maybe a song keeps running relentlessly through your head or one comes on the radio. When you hear the lyrics you'll find that it holds a message from me to you to remind you how I feel about you. You might want to get yourself a dream dictionary so you can refer to it when you see symbolic things in life on earth that shake you or in dreams that get your attention. If something demands your attention, it is usually a sign.

You keep saying that you want to see me in your dreams and yet you struggle with this. Don't you see I need you to believe in me. Could it be that you have been putting me in the past tense? Worried that other people will think you are crazy if you talk about me in the here and the now? Don't worry about what other people think. You should probably be selective as you share the fact that I am still alive, but I need you to have faith in me. Be sure to keep me in the present tense for if you put me in the past, you deny that I still exist and then you turn around and wonder why you don't see signs from me or see me in your dreams. Please don't deny me. I am here I am now. I am only gone from your sight. The following dream may help you to understand this:

Several times over the years Kate would tell me how she saw Grady in her dreams. In the dream Kate would say to her, "You can't be here, Grady, you died." Inevitably as she said that, Grady would disappear, poof, just like that. I tried to explain to her that she needed to accept Grady into her dreams. She needed to give Grady permission to stay. Until she did, Grady would have to honor what Kate believed to be true. When Kate said, "You can't be here," Grady could not stay. That's the way it works. A loyal dog obeys its master, even beyond the grave.

Reflections, Chapter 76

When you dream you go inside yourself, even though it may feel as if you are traveling many miles and light years to go to the dream worlds. This is the irony of all of it. Everything lives within the heart of the dreamer. Your heart can take you everywhere. It's the world where we are still together. The heart is where you'll find me and anyone else you have ever loved with all your heart and all your soul.

You might think that all dreams are signs. Sometimes they are and sometimes they aren't. Sometimes they are just "debris" from the day. Like a computer defragments what is taking up space, the mind sorts what needs to stay in your memory reserves and what needs to be filtered out. Sometimes dreams are places where you go to process your feelings about something. If you don't process things in your waking life, you are likely to do it in your dreams.

During your time of grief you might have tormenting thoughts that enter your dreams. These thoughts are almost always reflections of you. You might see me sick or injured or sad or frightened. You might even find that I die all over again. In actuality you are the one who is sick, sad, frightened. Injured. You are the one who is "dying" for you are the one who is no longer who you used to be. You likely have unresolved memories and feelings about me. That is why we are together in this kind of dream. A dream may keep coming back until you learn what it comes to teach you. What your higher self, your soul, has come to teach you. Sometimes it is none of these complex things at all. Sometimes a dream is just an opportunity for me to reach out to you. It allows me to come through the veil to you where I can be seen and felt. I can be close to you and give you a quick hug or a kiss and keep proving to you that my love for you is very much alive and well.

You are the dreamer. You are the creator of the dream. You are the dream. You know deep within your heart and soul why you have created it. You are trying to show yourself something. I am here to help you too. I will come if you invite me to join you and I will be whenever you need me to step in to reassure or protect you or to show you something that you need to know that you can't see for yourself. When you invite me, you open the door that was closed by your fear and barricaded by your grief.

When you fall asleep and dream, your mind overrides your physical brain. The brain is not your mind. When you go to sleep and leave the physical brain behind, your mind is free to travel anywhere without limitation. It's kind of what happens to people who are really good at meditation. It's kind of like what happened when I died and left my body. I found myself transported into a magical and unlimited world where anything can happen. The big difference now between you and me is that you have an invisible cord, like a leash, that harnesses you to Earth to be sure that when you dream, you can find your way back home. No matter where we are there is a system in place for all of us to be sure we can always find our way back home where we belong.

As I've said before, it's important to tell your story because what you don't share can remain unresolved. It can stay trapped inside of you and lurk around in the corners of your mind. You can even create nightmares for yourself. When nightmares come you are typically working things out in your subconscious. You will tend to project your own feelings onto everything and everyone that you see in your dreams. You are the one being tormented even though in your dream it seems like it is me. You are seeing yourself in everything. You are the one chasing. You are the one being chased. Many nightmares are really scary for you because they are based on your own fears about death and dying. Many of those longstanding fears are based on what people have told you about death and what you have seen in the movies and on TV. These dreams are trying to calm your fears and revamp your beliefs. They are trying to teach you new things based on truth and based on who you are now that you have grown in your faith and gained a new understanding through your healing.

If a dream bothers you or scares you, it's good to express it. If a dream keeps coming back to you over and over again, it's coming back for a reason. It has something to teach you. Maybe you can tell someone about it or keep a journal by your bedside. Write down your dreams and maybe someday when you look back on them you'll know what they came to tell you. Share it and let it go. Then allow the healing to begin in the space that you have created by letting it go.

You don't actually need to remember a dream for it to help you. Some of you are still waiting for the dream that will change your life. Ask for it, you might get it. Be sure to ask to remember it too for it is quite possible to have a wonderful dream one night and not be able to remember it in the morning. Keep in mind that your subconscious mind is processing and learning even when your conscious mind is asleep.

Don't forget to breathe. **BELIEVE.**

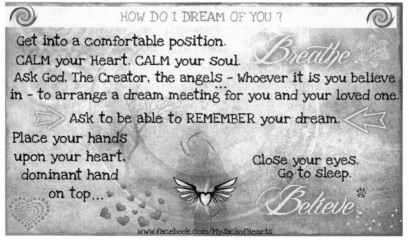

HOW DO I DREAM OF YOU ?

Get into a comfortable position.
CALM your Heart. CALM your Soul. *Breathe*
Ask God, The Creator, the angels - Whoever it is you believe in - to arrange a dream meeting for you and your loved one.

Ask to be able to REMEMBER your dream.

Place your hands upon your heart, dominant hand on top...

Close your eyes.
Go to sleep.

Believe

www.facebook.com/MyJackofHearts

SIGNS

Animal spirits often will appear during the hours between dusk and dawn; also known as the "tween times". They will always give you something. It may be just a simple pause within the chaos of life to remind you that there is more to life than the details of living it, working it and paying for it. It may be a shred of insight or a flash of recognition that comes to you in a fleeting thought or maybe in a dream in the tween times of your own mind.
The Lizard from Rainbow Bridge, Chapter 28

Many guides, angel messengers and animal spirits travel the world in the tween times. Coyotes are a good example. They typically come out just before nightfall and then again before the break of day. Other times too, but these are the times we can most easily reach you in spirit.

A "tween time" is when the difference between what is real (us) and what is illusion (the world you are living in) is blurred. The boundary has faded. My world and your world merge together. It is dusk, the day not over the night not yet begun. It is dawn, rising out of the night but still in the obscurity of twilight before the new day arrives. Your mind is more relaxed at these times; life is suspended in a type of harmonious balance, where yin meets yang. The tween times bring you right to the edge of the Rainbow. They can part the thin veil that separates you from me. They create a type of portal and when you practice recognizing them and tuning in, you can learn to connect with me more and more.

Many of you struggle to see the signs. Grief builds a wall that can keep us apart. Do you wonder why you can't see me, sense me, feel me? It's because when you weep and whine and brood and think yourself guilty when you are not, it pushes against my energy so I cannot reach you. When you have such an outpouring of emotion and sorrow, it's like me trying to swim upstream through a waterfall of tears to get to you. But if you can try to relax and have faith in me, I can sail right over to you on the calm waters of your soul.

Continually I am trying to communicate with you, trying to reach you through pictures, symbols, senses and emotional and physical "feelings." Another reason you haven't been able to see my signs may be because you haven't quite let go of me. You haven't allowed me to be free to be able to go where I want and need to go. Sometimes it seems to me that you want to keep me on an invisible leash because it makes you think that it is a clever way to "hold" me, but it really only holds me back from the freedom that is Heaven. I can't return to you until you let go of me in the first place. Once you are able to let go of me the miracles can happen. In the meantime I cannot return from a place I have not yet arrived, can I? You must let me go. The letting go takes place in your head because we are always connected at the heart. The letting go is not about letting go of the love. It's about letting go of the grief.

Sometimes I can make myself known and connect with you – in a dream, out of the corner of your eye. Sometimes you will feel me, hear me, or sense me although you may not necessarily see me there. That's because in that fleeting moment you are healthy and vibrating at a closer level to love; a closer vibration to what I am. Step out of your fear and into your love. If you vibrated in love all the time you would not have to ask if I am here with you, you would know beyond a doubt that I am here with you. Here and Now.

How do you know if it is a sign? How do you know if it's true? We are sending you signs all the time. When it happens unexpectedly...when something ordinary comes at an unusual time, in an unusual way or upon your request...when something happens that is extraordinary or difficult to fathom or explain, it is usually a sign.

Everything is connected to everything. Most of us animals are more tuned into the oneness of the universe than most humans are. Animal spirits walk the earth everywhere, every day. Angels are all around you. Protecting. Guiding. Loving you. Many of them you will not notice because you are too preoccupied to see them. Spirits always bring a gift. It may be a shred of insight or a flash of recognition that comes to you in a fleeting thought or maybe in a dream in the tween times of your mind.

I am telepathic. We all are. We always were. The word telepathic translates to "feeling across distance." It is how I understood you heart to heart when we lived upon the earth and it is how I now communicate with you from the heavenly realm. It's kind of like instantaneously being able to read one another's thoughts and feelings. It's how I know the thoughts you think and the feelings you are feeling. It is my greatest hope that I will be able to teach you to communicate on this level with me. You are telepathic too but you might not have known, but now you do. It's never too late to learn how to speak heart to heart, my heart to yours and yours to mine. I want to know what's on your heart not what's in your mind.

There may be someone else Here who is waiting to connect with you too. It's never too late to speak to someone on either side of the Bridge. If you are grieving a loss and regret that you did not say something to someone before they died, say it now. You can still connect with them. They are just waiting for you to invite them. I have come to teach you that relationships do not end. That you can communicate with someone long after earthly death. Love never dies. Put your hands on your heart and focus on the power there. Connect with them and tell them everything you've been waiting to share.

Your lack of faith and understanding of these dynamics that challenge everything you've learned have made it kind of hard to connect with me but you are learning even now how to do it. The other thing that has held you back is the lack of a balanced ability to receive. Humans are usually at one extreme or the other. They cannot receive because they do not feel worthy, or they do not know how to receive because they are so busy taking. Start now. Try to back off and allow others the time and space to give freely to you. Start thanking people for the gifts of their time, support or material things. Observe yourself in the moment. Are you greedy and eager? Do you struggle with self worth, perhaps even feeling guilty when someone gives you a gift? Are you afraid to trust because you fear they are keeping score and that you will owe them something? Even angels stop giving when they are not appreciated.

Start practicing the art of receiving. "Thank you!" for the compliment. "Thank you God for this day." "Thank you." "Thank you." It will not be long before you are thanking me for that rainbow or the dream that proves to you I still love you more than anyone else on earth.

Communication goes both ways. You need to be able to understand the signs and messages I send to you. It is through the heart that we see, hear and feel most clearly. It is like a radio signal. When it is strong the heart is like a megaphone and I get your message loud and clear. You message echoes throughout the universe when it comes from the heart on the wings of intention and faith. It is the most direct line of communication in existence once you filter out the "interference" of worry and doubt in your head, the thoughts that don't matter and only serve to block the reception. Your intention is the force, love is the connection and faith is the key that opens the door between you and me.

I sent her reminders of me. I sent her clouds shaped like me and trees that whispered my name as she passed by. Then one day she heard my dog tags jingling on the trail. Soon after that she saw my face in the patterns of her curtains and also in the clouds that passed in front of the moon. She thought when she saw these things that she was going crazy, but she was not crazy. She just didn't realize that the messages were coming from me.

Reflections, Chapter 72

You know how it feels. To want to see to touch to feel again. I want you as much as you want me, if not more. I long to reach you. I express myself to you through thoughts, feelings and pictures in my mind. I try to forecast the pictures of my thoughts to you but it's difficult. You have learned to second-guess yourself because of what other people have told you. When I send my thoughts into your mind, you think they are your thoughts and you cast them aside with disregard, thinking they are 'crazy' thoughts of your own, not knowing they are mine! Not knowing that they are not crazy at all. On the contrary. They are more sane and pure and honest and true than most of the thoughts that you are thinking.

Sometimes your mind and thoughts are just too scattered and full of other things to realize that I am right here inside with you, speaking to you from within your own thoughts. But don't worry about it. We'll both get better at this in the days ahead.

The one thing that seems to work pretty well for us on this side ---and it's really fun too--- is when we take a special symbol that carries an important message and we create it in 3D for you in your world. We take advantage of your five senses because you can't deny what your eyes see, what your ears hear, what your fingers touch. These symbols can stop you in your tracks.

160

Perhaps a beautiful rainbow will light up the darkened sky or a feather waits for you to find it on your path. It's up to me to find clever ways to reach out to you. Watch for me. I will also present myself in things that are associated with power and energy like light bulbs, clocks, electronics and appliances. Electricity is the closest thing on earth to what I became when I crossed Rainbow Bridge so it's pretty easy for me to reach you through similar energy circuits.

Do you ever get goose bumps? Goose bumps are kind of like an electrical sensation on your skin. Pay attention to them for they are the tangible evidence of vibrational presence. If you have goose bumps you know that whatever you are thinking, feeling or saying must be true. Have you ever been with a friend and said something only to have them reply, "That gave me goose bumps!" or "Wow, that gives me the chills." That's their way of telling you that what you said to them is true. Goose bumps are like truth detector machines. Goose bumps are not just a random occurrence. They are how I can reach out to you in vibration. It's one way I can reach out and touch you.

There may come a time when you might sense the millions of angels too small to be witnessed, like fairies that live in the curve of a leaf or who sleep under the tiniest rose petal.
Return from Rainbow Bridge, Chapter 33

HOW TO TELL THE CHILDREN
AND COMFORT YOUR REMAINING PET

Please don't hide death or your tears from your two legged or four legged children. Both heal faster than most adults do. The passage of "time" in the mind of a child or a pet makes little sense at all. Time is just an illusion. Most children and pets are living in the moment and they heal very quickly because of it.

Believe it or not, in the scheme of things, this is actually a positive lifetime learning experience for your children. Adults who have not experienced death directly when they were younger can be quite disabled when it happens when they are older. Remember how I said that grief is a good teacher? It will not be long and you will see that you will all be better and the family stronger for having known and loved me. Already the kids are developing the tools and intuition that they need to start building their ability to handle grief and loss in the future. It is an important tool to have in a world that brings the guarantee of loss the longer one lives.

When all earth-beings are born they enter the world like all of us do, whether we have four legs or two. For a little while after we are born we still remember where we come from and where it's all leading. Much like animals, babies cannot speak of it because they don't yet have the language skills to do so. It's all by design, for they are not born to come and tell their parents all the secrets of the universe their parents have long forgotten. They have other means of communication, as you all too well know. Many of them will cry and cry and cry because they remember the world they have come from and it is so much sweeter and softer than this new one they have been born into. Through the early years they have to go through their own period of grief. They have had to let go of the perfect world they lived in to come into this imperfect one. The terrible twos by the way, are just the final letting go as they realize and accept that they will be staying here on earth for a while and That's That!

"My other pet is grieving too..."

Yes your remaining pet may grieve for a short while but remember, our lives spin seven times faster than yours and we heal seven times faster too. You might get upset from time to time when your pet seems to exhibit certain behaviors or feelings but chances are they are just reflections of you and your grief. Like those of us within your dreams, we are usually showing you YOU. If you think we look sad, we are showing you that you are sad. If we seem angry or restless, take a look at yourself and see if it reflects how you are feeling at the time. If you are still trying to release the memory of my frightened and pained face before the time of my passing, it is likely I was fully focused and tuned in, reflecting you in those moments. I was not frightened, but you were. Your face was pained. You were the anxious one. Since we are connected at the heart through life and through life after death, I know how you feel and I show you in each and every moment.

We learn as we grow, learning the rules and standards of behavior from you. Children, as they grow early on, learn by copying their parents and other role models in their lives. Life can be a hall of mirrors, reflections everywhere you turn. When your heart is pained when you see your young child crying and you think your child is grieving, please keep this in mind: Often the underlying reason for the tears is that your child sees you crying and he is learning that this is the appropriate response to losing someone you love. Depending on his age, it is more likely that he is copying or mimicking you than actually feeling the pain that brings tears. He is learning the ropes of living life from you. He is witnessing by your actions how to cope with grief. So far, the only way he knows how to live is to copy how you live. Consider this in all that you do. The children are watching you all the time so that when they grow up to live their own lives they will know how to do it and teach their own children how to do it because they had you as their teacher. Make sure you are a good one.

You need each other now. Stay open and honest. Be loving. They will help you process and help you heal if you just keep your heart open. Pets and kids can see things that most adult human beings cannot. Don't laugh at them if they say they see me there. Their eyesight is still pure, their minds open and their natural intuition still intact. They live closer to the edge of Tween Time than you do. Their minds have not yet created interference; the signals and messages are still clear.

This time of grief is an opportunity for you to see how they rise to the occasion. Their innate wisdom might even surprise you. It's yet another gift of discernment. Don't be surprised if when you're trying to come up with the right words to say to comfort them, they find the right words to comfort you instead. Some children have said very profound and insightful things to their adults during grief. Let them teach you what you need to remember.

Pay close attention, for children often will act things out during their play. There is a type of counseling called Creative Play Therapy. It allows children the space and time to work things out during playtime. They do not need a therapist present to do play therapy, although if your child seems to struggle too much for too long it is an option to explore. Most simply need the time and space to be allowed to play freely without being judged. Many adults who now struggle emotionally never had the opportunity or were given permission to play their way through their childhood challenges and issues. Children can play alone or with each other, it doesn't matter. Healing comes naturally through their play because they still remember how to intrinsically heal. They are still in tune with their heart and soul and they know their pain and confusion needs to be resolved through the expression of it. Play is how they sort it out. They can paint or write or dance. Any form of creative expression or social game can be effective. Because most aren't yet well versed in speaking their feelings, young kids must play them out symbolically. Some children can say some pretty profound things when they are serving their teddy bear tea at the tea table or their soldiers are waiting for their next command in the sandbox. They know inherently that strong feelings need to be expressed at the time they are feeling them. They still speak and understand the language of the heart. Always try to accept them and praise their insight, for they will carry your praise for their gifts of Knowing forward – and become wise, intuitive, insightful adults.

When you were pregnant did anyone explain to you that you could speak to your child within the womb? Did you know that they could feel your feelings from deep inside? That they could feel your love for them or the lack thereof? Your child knew well in advance if you wanted them or not. Souls are connected one to the other in invisible ways. The only difference now is that there is no connection by umbilical cord but still connected nonetheless through the mutual power of the love in your hearts and your souls.

Always talk to your child or your pet heart to heart even if you think they are too young to understand. The power of your words and the emotions that fuel them will reach them at the deepest level. Create a calm, nurturing, comfortable space. Bring all the love you can summon into your voice, your eyes, and your loving arms. Cry with them. Talk to them like you would talk to a very dear friend. Tell them you are learning about healing too, that you miss me very much and you know that they do too. Bring up happy memories of me. Reassure them that things will get better. Tell them everything and then allow them the quiet space for them to "talk" to you. It may sound crazy but it is healing at the basic power level of the heart that understands everything no matter how many legs and no matter what age or ability.

Your child and your remaining pet are there for good reason. You need them and they need you too. You are beginning to create an important line of communication for yourselves and your family. Your child is learning things from this experience that will create a maturity, acceptance and level of grace that will carry on throughout life. Loss ultimately makes you strong if you've handled it wisely and if you lose someone you love when you are young, that strength prevails and compassion becomes part of your character.

Don't force anything. Tell them it's okay to cry, to be angry, to feel confused, to feel sad and that it's okay to feel okay again, because they will. Talk to them about me. Read great books and watch uplifting and educational movies together so that they learn about death and rebirth. Tell them about Rainbow Bridge and how we'll all meet again one day. Don't be afraid to cry for it teaches them that all tears serve a purpose. Reassure them that I am waiting patiently for all of you, Only Gone from your Sight. Explain to them that they might even see me, hear me, or feel me now and then. Tell them how much you need each other now. Reassure them that you will all heal as a family and that someday soon you will feel the love and not the pain and when and if it's appropriate for you, that I will lead you all to another special friend.

Comfort them and reassure them that they are not alone. Listen to the words you say. The very words you say to them are the very words you need to hear. Humans tend to give each other what they themselves need. So tell them these important things and then turn around and tell them to your very own heart.

LIFE BEYOND GRIEF
LOVING AGAIN

It had been a divine set up. My Master sent me to her to teach her how wonderful it is to love and be loved so that when I was gone from her she would yearn for love again. She would no longer be afraid of love. She would one day realize that the love we shared was her reward for taking a chance on love, for taking a chance on me.

Return from Rainbow Bridge, Chapter 57

I see you. I feel your heart. I know why you are lonely. You're lonely because I taught you to love...but you see I couldn't stay forever. I taught you to love because once you love like that you don't know how to live your life without it. I taught you so that you would miss love so much that you would want to find it again. I taught you because I want you to be happy again and to have a beautiful life. I taught you because it's love that makes life worthwhile and if anyone deserves a beautiful life, it's you.

Maybe it doesn't seem fair to you that we do not live a human lifetime. Most of us will come and go in 4 years, 7 years, 12 years, 16, less or more, maybe even 20 if we're lucky. Horses can go a little longer. Maybe you will do this 1 or 2 or 3 more times in your life...if you are willing to risk loving again.

Have you thought about getting another pet? Do you ask yourself: "Can I bear to go through this again? Should I get another pet? If so, when?" Only you know the answer to this. Don't let anyone try to tell you what is best for you. You are the one who knows best. There will always be people who are happy to tell you what they think you should do. What works for one person might not work for another. Do what YOU think you should do.

Early in your grief I heard you announce to others indignantly, "I'm never getting another pet!" I know you said it amidst the deepest pain of your grief, but how do you think that makes me feel? It makes me think that maybe I brought you more pain than joy. If you had me for 15 years and it took three days to lose me, why would you not be willing to love again? Maybe you just aren't up to having a pet right now. Maybe you're too exhausted from the grieving and the growing. Maybe you are still angry. You can always volunteer at a shelter or offer to take care of other people's pets until you have more time to recover. Don't write us off just yet. Based on what you say, you aren't quite healed all the way.

If you want to overcome pain from the past, bring in new life for the future...but only when the time is right. The most important thing you can do is relax about it and Do Not Force Anything. When you are forcing something that doesn't feel right then it isn't right. What is meant to be yours will come.

As you heal you'll feel things begin to shift in your heart. It's my love at work. It's evidence that I am still there with you. You'll find yourself developing stronger relationships with your children and your remaining pets. If you don't have a pet, you might find yourself starting to think about getting another. It is a strange human tendency to feel guilty thinking these thoughts but there is nothing to feel guilty about. It's life. It's loss. It's growth and it's transformation. It's all about love.

Your own voice inside your head will keep you quite busy. "...But it's too soon..." "Won't my old pet be jealous?" "What will people think of me?" "My heart tells me YES but my mind says NO." Ah, there's your answer.

If your heart is telling you it's time to love again, listen to it. It always tells the truth. I am in your heart and I am the one who is telling you. With my Heavenly Master's help, I direct the desires of your heart. I direct you so that you are in the right place at the right time for that which is right for you. It may be a week, it may be a year, or less or more. Don't try to judge it or plan it out. I know what you need better than anyone does and I am in the position to bring it to you when you are ready. When the time is right I will guide you to the right one.

I want you to love again. Someone who needs you is waiting for you; someone yet unknown who waits patiently but desperately for you, for the love waiting in your heart, to be given and received.

We have a special friend. He has had horses, dogs and cats all of his life since he was a boy down on the family farm. I think the number is 21 pets over the course of his life so far. Every time one dies, he runs out immediately before the shock wears off to get another. Some say he is doing it too soon. Some label him "impulsive". They feel he should take more time to think about it before acting on it. The fact is, he knows what he's doing. It works for him. He doesn't need time to think, he just needs time to feel. He's been through loss enough times to know exactly what he's doing.

"I do it to honor the life of the one I just lost," he says. Imagine if he were still deliberating whether or not to get another pet. He would never have had 21 rounds of love stories with no doubt more to come, God willing. Pets can keep their best two-legged friends healthier longer. Aside from obvious social perks, pets are good for the heart, the blood pressure, depression prevention and stress relief.

I am not telling you that this is how you should do it because everyone is different. What I will ask of you is to consider adopting another pet when the time is right for you, because it will honor me. Because I'm the one who taught you how to love more than you ever did before.

"Don't you think I am too old for another pet?" you ask.

Geraldine was 90. She had lost her only daughter and lived alone at home with her 10 year old Shih Tzu. They were the best of friends but when her dog passed unexpectedly, Geri immediately called Kate to help her locate a new pet. They found Buddy, a three-year old poodle that had been abused, turned into the kill shelter and then saved by a local rescue group. The two had shared three wonderful years together when Geri had to say goodbye to Buddy when she went into hospice care. She predeceased him.

Because of Geri's willingness to love again and again, she had had 30 pets over her 90 years. 30 hellos, 30 goodbyes, and 30 more angels waiting for her at the edge of the Rainbow Bridge. Buddy now lives very comfortably with Geri's best friend. It worked out really well because Geri and Buddy and her friend always spent so much time together that it was quite easy for Buddy to adjust to it all after Geri was gone. Please don't hesitate to get another pet no matter what your age. Just plan ahead so that you have someone nearby to help when you can't do it all and who will be happy to take them into their home if you are taken home to Heaven first.

Geri knew. Each and every pet is different and you can never replace a pet with a new one and have the same experience you had before. That's the beauty of it. Each pet teaches you new kinds of lessons and each lesson is always about a new kind of love.

You are never too old to love again. In fact you have more to offer than ever, based on the wisdom of your years. Just make your choices wisely based on who you are now. If you have trouble walking around the block, don't get a hound that needs a lot of exercise unless you have a big fenced-in yard. Get a lapdog or a cat that can get plenty of exercise just running around the house or on a slow and gentle walk through the neighborhood. Consider a 7-pound pet rather than a 70-pound pet. Keep your eyes open for a five-year-old not a five month old. Be sure, like Geri did, to put a plan in your will that includes directives where your new pet will go if you die first.

You think I'll be upset if you live to love again? Why, I came here to teach you love! What good is learning something if you never use it? I'm asking you to love again.

I know you are still grieving the loss of me. I know that I was your very best friend. I want you to be happy above all and somewhere there is someone else who needs you. So many are waiting for a good home like the one you gave to me. They are waiting in shelters and foster homes. Perfectly healthy loving pets are facing their final hours in kill shelters. You could make a difference in the life of the one who needs you. The one who is waiting for love to walk through the door. Waiting to be chosen. Waiting to surprise you with how much love they have to give to you.

As you wait for your new friend to come into your life, never ever try to duplicate me for you will be dealt a hand you never planned on. When you try to keep things the "same," you will be given a whole new set of challenges. You will look at the one who looks like me and say, "Why can't you be more like ___?" because when they look like me you subconsciously expect them to act like me and they are not me. It is not fair to yourself or to your new pet. Plus, think about it from my point of view. "Is she trying to replace me?" Just no. Same breed is okay. If you HAPPEN to fall in love with one that HAPPENS to resemble me, well, okay. Let your heart lead the way, not your eyes and your desire to keep things the same.

I am not where you are looking. Don't agonize about it. The pet that's meant to be with you will simply arrive at the right time. You'll find yourself in the right place. You'll feel the certainty in your heart. That's how you'll know it will be yours.

There is something that tends to happen for many of you. Sometimes you think you've found the right one. You fall in love quickly. You are sure this is The One. Oh you can hardly wait to start this new chapter of love! You prepare to bring them home. Scared and excited, you find yourself already quite attached to them. Then something happens and it doesn't work out. You cry because you have invested so much of yourself in this process. You were so sure! You say "Why?"

Why? Because that one did you a favor. These are your teachers too. They were put in your life by design. They either led you to the Right One that you would not have found otherwise, or they healed something inside of you that still needed healing before you could be ready to commit to love again. Do not judge what seems to be unfortunate. It is by design. The heart guides you every step of the way. We guide you. We know exactly what you need and when.

When new love comes to you I will not envy because I know that no one takes my place with you. I'm in your heart and there I'll stay. I'll wait without condition and I will love the ones you come to love.
Reflections, Chapter 88

Try not to feel guilty for another moment about this. I am not jealous. I love you and my love is true. All I want is for you to be happy again. I don't want you to feel alone anymore.

You ask, "When...When will the crying end? When will the grieving end? When will I look at my new pet and not just miss the one I used to have?"

Believe me when I tell you this. It will just take a little time and you will one day find that all your loves have merged together. You will be surprised because you will find yourself laughing or smiling over a memory of me and that's when you will know that your tears will soon subside. I want you to be free to love again and to be happy when you are reminded of me! You'll get there, you'll see, and it will be sweet and beautiful with a few sentimental tears now and again for all the loves you have had.

My Friend. You can't replace me.
But you can bring in a new kind of love
...a new kind of pet.
You've had her now for several months.
You see that she is healing. You feel yourself
healing too. You are healing each other. It has taken
this long for you to trust each other.
She no longer runs from you. She now comes to you
seeking your love. Seeking the new level of love that
I taught you to give. You are healed enough now to
give her everything and more. But I know.
I know you still love me. I still see you cry
When you don't think you have everything...
But you do.
You have her. You have me.
You do have everything.

ONLY HUMAN

"It bothers me so much when others say, 'I know exactly how you feel'...when others say, 'Just get another puppy.'" "You can rescue!"

No one knows another's pain. Some will suggest that you replace me as soon as possible to fill the emptiness you feel. They don't know that it is much more than just emptiness that you feel. Most people typically don't know what to say to soothe your grief, on the contrary. Sometimes they say things that make you feel worse. Their intentions are good but they don't know how much it hurts you at this point to hear some of these words and overused phrases.

Some people sacrifice lifelong friendships because of one careless thing said in haste in the time of grief. Now is not a good time for burning bridges. You have suffered enough loss for the time being. Don't bring any more onto yourself. Try not to cut too many ties during the most challenging times of grief. Try to understand why they might not understand. There is always a reason. If you have had a friend for 30 years and they say something thoughtless, it would be best to forgive them the error and revisit it at a later time when you can see more clearly when you are not operating under the burden of grief. You can always revisit it later if it still bothers you. Don't place any value on what someone says who doesn't value the love of a pet. This person does not know love. This person lives by a different set of rules. If you do anything, pity them for they do not know what true love is.

It happens to everyone to an extent. Let's say they see you from Day #1 when you are still in shock from your loss. Maybe you are despondent, withdrawn. Some time later they witness your anger, passive or active, they feel their own discomfort with the anger. Then the depression. They don't realize it is yet another stage. They don't know about the five stages of grief the way you do. They just think you've been "depressed" from the moment of loss. They see it go on and on and they might think that you've been depressed (in their estimation) for quite a long time now; they think maybe you should be getting over it or maybe you need to be "fixed".

"Maybe you shouldn't talk about it now," they say as if to protect you. They are actually trying to protect themselves from the distress of not knowing how to help you. "You know how upset you get." Or they speak in clichés which may be true but sound callous and shallow like, "It's God's Plan" "Well you still have another one." "Aww Heaven must've needed a beautiful angel!" These words offer little consolation. There are plenty of people who will step up to the plate and profess to be an expert in an effort to "help" you. They are not experts. They do not know how to handle their own stress and losses. Their intentions may be good but you must take their comments with a grain of salt and not take them to heart. You don't need to be fixed. You aren't broken. You are working your way through the process of grief.

A lot of people run the other way and close their eyes to the pain. They do not want to feel your pain so they avoid you. You think they are being uncaring but the fact is they are afraid of your pain and your sorrow. They may care for you deeply but they do not have depth enough or understanding enough to talk with you on common ground. A lot of people "shut down" in a time of crisis. All of you are being put to the test and unless you are a counselor, seasoned grief survivor or spiritual guru, you are not always able to do or say the best thing for someone under the circumstances.

If you are looking for support from someone and it doesn't seem to come, it's not always that they are thoughtless or uncaring. Some people simply do not have the depth of feeling. Some do not have the courage to be with you in your time of grief. There are some who simply don't experience great levels of emotion and they can come across cool and aloof. Try to be patient with them and accept the fact that some humans are simply not capable of understanding the way you feel, for one reason or another.

One of the things I came to teach you is unconditional love. Love of yourself and of others. Non-judgment, acceptance, no expectations, forgiveness. Ask yourself, if you encounter a seemingly insensitive friend, what I would do if I were you? How would you handle it if you were

181

me? What would you say to me if they were me? Try to see it from all angles. Hold yourself in the space of unconditional love the way I would. An important part of being unconditional is accepting a person where they're at and loving them anyway. Not to say you shouldn't end a relationship if it has been historically abusive or hurtful. It's not about tolerating being treated without kindness and respect. It's about accepting a relationship for what it is and not having unrealistic expectations that only aggravate and disappoint.

One of Kate's most well-meaning friends, one who had known me and supposedly loved me, said upon hearing the news of my death, "It's going to be okay Kate. Life will be easier now. It's very expensive and a lot of work to have a dog." Another uttered the popular and ultimate insult, "It's just a dog. You can get another one." "Gosh," said another, "You've been grieving quite a long time. Maybe you need to see a counselor or get yourself some Xanax." There are many well-intended, normally intelligent people who simply don't have a clue about what to say when someone grieves. Maybe some day they will learn when they go through a significant loss of their own. After all, life is our teacher and they are still learning too. Even the ones who think they know it all. Especially them.

At the beginning of grief when emotions rage, try to minimize your losses. If you are not ready to talk about it, don't. It's okay to tell people you aren't ready to talk about it. You still have healing to do before you can consider all of the alternatives. When the time is right, however, it's important to feel your feelings and express them to those who understand and accept you. Share your sadness and your upset with someone who really cares about you.

Because you have learned discernment from the grief, you can choose your friends wisely. You can thoughtfully look at the friends you have and know who will support you the most. If your friend/s once welcomed you into their home and their life and welcomed me too, it's a good sign. If they only wanted you and not me, then it's a sign too. They will welcome you with your grief if they welcomed you and me. They will probably not understand your grief if they did not accommodate or appreciate your relationship with me when I was living. Go only where we both will be honored and welcomed: you and your grief. And me.

Most people nowadays live in their busy minds. They think too much and don't love enough. Maybe they've come from dysfunctional families and never learned to communicate their feelings or what they want or what they need. You may be one of them which makes this all the much harder to not isolate yourself. It's so sad; so many people don't even know what they are missing. Perhaps they never had a pet that came into their world to continually remind them of what is most important: the love that lives in their hearts, not the busy thoughts in their heads.

Grief slows everything down so that you can focus on you. If you have always been a supportive person, there for others in their times of need, you will experience additional discomfort from having the shoe on the other foot. You simply cannot be there for others when you need to take care of yourself and yet you might not know how to act

183

because you never really needed anyone before. You were never not there for someone in need. Now that Someone is you and you need to take care of you.

One of the gifts grief can bring to you is to weed out your garden of friendship and show you who your true friends are. Take inventory of the flowers that are left when the weeds are gone. Leave space and room in your garden for new friends to bloom so you can grow together, learning as you move forward into a new season of life.

GRIEF SUPPORT

We are all lost souls until we are found.

Every loving family struggles with the loss of their pet. Loss can be especially difficult if you live alone with little or no family support. It is often the single, the aged, the disabled and retired who struggle the most; those who are now alone, live alone, feel alone. After all, I was your "family," your "therapist," your "go to" whenever you needed love and support. I was always there for you. If you are vulnerable or perhaps I have even been your service animal, you will tend to suffer harder and longer than others because not only have you lost your best friend, you have lost a consistent supporter, a reliable nurturer and a protective partner. On the other hand, if you have a balanced life and are surrounded by caring family and supportive friends, chances are you will have an easier time of it. No matter what your circumstances, you will have to work through the grief of losing me.

If you have been repeatedly rejected, hurt or disillusioned by your experiences with other people, you may search for a safer route to love. You may find yourself taking the safest route of all, which is to make your relationship with your pet your primary relationship. After all, you will get 100% guaranteed unconditional love and support! The problem comes when it's time to say goodbye. You can become desperate, feeling you are losing everything that matters. You look around for support and you see little, if any. It's very important in the scheme of your life to plan to have a few good two-legged friends when it's time for me to cross the bridge, so that you have human friends there to support you. No one can do it alone. Not even you.

Another scenario seems to come up sadly and repeatedly. It is worse than just being alone. If you have a partner or spouse who doesn't understand or teases or disrespects or abuses you during your grief over losing me, put your new power of discernment to work. Think twice whether you want to spend much more time with this person. However, do not act in haste. Remember not to make major decisions too quickly during times of grief. You cannot yet see clearly, which can cause you to be supersensitive and result in outcomes that you may regret later.

Sometimes well-meaning humans can become jealous of the kind of relationship you have had with me. They have seen you day in and day out give me so much warmth and attention while they hang out on the fringe, watching, waiting, getting more and more upset when you don't offer them the same care and affection that you've given me. They can attack you when you are at your most vulnerable and they will then show you their true feelings. Remember, their anger is typically a cover-up for fear and insecurity. I'm sorry if that has happened to you but it is the gift of insight that grief gives to you so you can see the truth about someone. Once you know how they really feel, you can decide together if you need to work on your relationship to make it better or if it's time to move on. It is a gift given to you so that you can make the very best decisions for yourself, now and in the future.

If you don't have anyone you feel comfortable turning to for support, take a look at formal supports in your community. Join a local pet loss support group or hospice bereavement group. If you belong to a church, visit the pastor or minister for support and guidance. There are also established online groups like our Facebook Heart to Heart support group.

Sometimes you must go outside of your circle of friends and family to find the best connection. In just the click of a button, if you choose your group wisely, you will have a built-in family of people and more new friends than you can fathom. Friends who will understand, accept and support you in this common shared experience. There is nothing more powerful than coming face to face with someone who has experienced a similar loss. You look into their eyes and you know that they are like you in this way. You know they understand.

It's never too soon to open up your life to new friends who are kind and caring. It's never too soon or too late to ask for support. Later when you rise from the ashes of your grief, you will find you have even more to offer others than you ever did before. You may even find yourself reaching out in ways that are helpful to others who are going through the same thing.

Many of our pet loss support group members came laden with their 'broken hearts.' All they could see at the time was their loss and their pain and their hopeless suffering. Over time, however, they healed, rising up in faith and now many continue to support and guide others who struggle to rise above their pain. Sharing the wisdom of your experience with the newly grieving shows you the contrast of your own grief and survival and it teaches you how much you have learned and how much more you have to share. You are now strong enough and compassionate enough to reach out to help others. Because you understand. You've been there too. You know what to say to them.

~I'm sorry for your loss.
~This must be really hard for you.
~I've lost someone too but I can't imagine what it must be like for you.
~Do you want to talk about it?
~Is there something I can do for you?
~It doesn't seem fair.
~It's okay to cry.
~Oh you're not crazy at all, it's the grief. Here, let's read this book together!
~Grief is temporary. This too shall pass. You'll be okay once you work through this.
~I love you.

It's so true what they say that you can't love someone else until you love yourself. Supporting others can be very healing and rewarding but be sure you are stable before you extend yourself too much. Without boundaries you may find yourself falling back into your own grief and also grieving constantly because you find yourself living within the grief of others... because you cannot separate your grief from theirs. It's like a recovering alcoholic who stops drinking but replaces the alcohol with another addiction. When the depth of grief is still there, you can simply switch over, immerse yourself into the grief of others and then voila, you have the combined grief of everyone to contend with. There is a condition known as Compassion Fatigue. Without strong boundaries, taking care of others at your own expense will deplete and exhaust you and fill your mind with fodder when it needs to be clear. Also by focusing on others it will continue to keep you out of your very own heart.

An "empath" is one who feels another's emotions as one's own. Those who are empathetic are particularly susceptible to burning out when supporting others. If you are an empath, please be certain to take care of yourself by protecting yourself from taking on the pain of other people. Sometimes when you have healed from a grief you thought would never end, you want to save others from going through similar pain. You cannot save them, nor should you. They need to walk through the valley of the shadow by themselves and there is a power much greater than you that will help them through it. Without walking through their own fire of grief, they will never learn what you have learned. If Kate had not been alone when she experienced the last week of my demise and the dark period that followed, she would not have learned what she learned. There would be no books, no Jack McAfghan. The only way people can get stronger is by going through the hurdles of the stages of grief on their own, with support. As they say: the fire purifies. The grit forms the pearl. What doesn't destroy us strengthens us.

Intuition is a wonderful gift but it can be both a blessing and a curse. If you can easily tune in to the grief of another, it is very easy to lose your way if you have not yet resolved your own present or past trauma and grief. If you have not healed from your own grief and you turn around and give all you have to give, you will find yourself drowning. Soon there will be nothing left of you. You will crash and then build yourself up until you crash again. The key is in finding the balance to avoid the crash. Pull back when you begin to feel stressed. It's up to you to learn your limits, respect them and give just enough to others without giving too much. Believe it or not, it's part of your growth. Grief is still teaching you to recognize the signs so someday you will pay attention to how you feel so you can learn to set boundaries for yourself and have a more balanced and healthy life.

Kate used to cry as her patients cried and as their families cried. She was empathetic and she had a very hard time separating herself from their pain. The fact is that Kate had some unresolved losses and issues hiding out deep beneath her clinical competence. These issues made it difficult for her to set boundaries and to not experience their pain as if it were her own. She thought it was their pain but it was really hers.

It's not up to you to cure the others. It's up to you to give a listening ear and give them the resources they need to help themselves. Always take time for you so that you can continue to help others. Always save plenty of energy for yourself. If you haven't learned anything else from me, remember this: You are the most important person of all.

Don't offer advice. Don't tell them what to do. Just be fully present with them. Just like I taught you to be with me. Don't tell them how they should be feeling. Just give them permission to feel whatever they feel and to express it. Heart to heart. All feelings are accepted and appropriate. Don't take things personally. Validate them. Fill them with certain hope that they will heal and that life will be good again. After all, you are living proof!

After reading this book you understand more about death than most people who grieve or who love someone who grieves. What better person to offer love and understanding than someone who's been through the trenches too? You. You've been through it and you're coming out of it a beautiful New You. I know I've said it before; I am so proud of you.

There may be places in this book where I may sound like I think I am God. I am not God. No one can be God but we are all pieces of God. All of us are His representatives. All angels are offshoots of the One who first created them. All of us resonate at His level of love and we speak His truth. It's all By Design. He wants us to exemplify what He is and He wants us to share His truth: the truth that we share in this book. The book was written in the hopes that more people will heal their hearts and souls by learning the truth. Discovering the truth and gaining knowledge will help dissipate all the

191

fears you have about death and maybe even some you have about life. Life is too short, and too long, to live in fear.

Love lives forever. Souls live forever. Every living breathing thinking being has a soul. It is a matter of time. You will die. Those you love will die. It is the luck of the draw who will die first. Will you be the griever or the cause for the grief? You can't plan for anything. You won't know anything until it happens.

Live your life so that when you die, you will be celebrated for having lived. Live your life so that when others die, you can rise from the ashes of grief and live life renewed from what they have taught you. From what grief has taught you. From what I have taught you. Treat those living as well as you treat those who are dying. Live Heart to Heart with the faith that life is the school, love is the lesson and that love never dies.

And one day, in time that will pass
in the blink of an eye, I will meet you at the gate
and we will run together through the soft green
meadow into a beautiful new world.
Reflections, Chapter 88

ALL THE LOVE YOU EVER GAVE WAITS FOR YOU AT RAINBOW BRIDGE.

THE END....
Is just the beginning...

Neither death nor life, neither angels nor demons, neither our fears for today nor our worries about tomorrow—not even the powers of hell can separate us.
Romans 8:38

WHEN SOMEONE YOU LOVE IS DYING

1. Tell them you love them love them love them.
2. Acknowledge what is happening now. They need someone to share in their experience of Life's Final Stage of Growth.
3. Let them know in no uncertain terms that they are free to go. Be sure to tell them you will miss them.
4. Thank them for all they did for you – even if it was to teach you patience, tolerance or not to take things personally.
5. Hold their hand. Don't be afraid to touch them. Death is not contagious.
6. Ask them to send you a sign after they get where they're going. Ask them to come into your dreams or tell them some other specific way you would like them to show up in your life.
7. If they are nearing death, prioritize them. Take time off from work. Cancel your dates, your family vacation. This will help you to relieve the guilt that always comes when they are gone.
8. Live in the moment with them. Put your smartphone away. Look into their eyes even if you have never done that before in your life together with them. It is the eyes that hold the memories of the soul.
9. Communicate with them from your heart. When they are gone from your sight it is not your mouths and your ears but your hearts that will communicate one to the other.
10. Remind yourself that they are not "dead." They live on in another form in another place not far from you.

BLESS THEM AND LET THEM GO.

If you enjoyed this book, you may be asked to leave a review. Please do because it's your reviews that keep us going! They keep us writing! You make it possible for other readers to find Jack's healing message too. *THANK YOU!*

We invite you to visit our Heart to Heart pet loss support group at
www.facebook.com/groups/edgeoftherainbow

Our Signs and Messages group at
www.facebook.com/groups/rainbowsandfeathers

Follow Jack's Blog at
www.jackmcafghan.com
and connect with him on Facebook
www.facebook.com/MyJackofHearts

If you continue to struggle with grief and loss, please seek out a qualified bereavement or loss counselor to help you through it. Most local hospice organizations have a trained social worker or pastor available who provides services in the community at low or no charge. Find others grieving in pet loss support groups. National Volunteer Agencies can help. More and more Pet Clinics are offering support services. Connect with a pet hospice group if you are fortunate enough to have one in your area. Feel free to visit Kate's website for these and other resources.

Author Kate McGahan has been a hospice grief counselor and clinical social worker for over 35 years. The first book in the Jack McAfghan Trilogy was released in 2015 and there are more books and genres forthcoming.

Kate brings stories to her readers in an entertaining and thought-provoking way. When you learn something new you grow, when you grow you heal. It's By Design. She writes each and every book to heal something in the reader. While you think she is just entertaining you, she is also planting seeds and teaching you new ways of looking at yourself and those you love.

Death is like turning the final page in a book you've come to love. But it's not over. It's never over. Stay tuned for more books and subscribe to author updates at www.katemcgahan.com

Godspeed your journey.

Made in the USA
Middletown, DE
26 December 2020